Relationships Within Ecosystems

elevate science
MODULES

You're an author!

As you write in this science book, your answers and personal discoveries will be recorded for you to keep, making this book unique to you. That is why you are one of the primary authors of this book.

In the space below, print your name, school, town, and state. Then write a short autobiography that includes your interests and accomplishments.

YOUR NAME ....

SCHOOL ....

TOWN, STATE ....

AUTOBIOGRAPHY ....

....

Your Photo

Savvas Learning Company LLC, 15 East Midland Avenue, Paramus, NJ 07652

The cover photo shows a butterfly on white flowers.

Front cover: Butterfly, Eirini Karapostoli/EyeEm/Getty Images; Back cover: Science Doodle, LHF Graphics/Shutterstock.

ISBN-13: 978-1-418-29157-0
ISBN-10: 1-418-29157-9
5 20

Program Authors

ZIPPORAH MILLER, EdD
Coordinator for K-12 Science Programs, Anne Arundel County Public Schools
Dr. Zipporah Miller currently serves as the Senior Manager for Organizational Learning with the Anne Arundel County Public School System. Prior to that she served as the K-12 Coordinator for science in Anne Arundel County. She conducts national training to science stakeholders on the Next Generation Science Standards. Dr. Miller also served as the Associate Executive Director for Professional Development Programs and conferences at the National Science Teachers Association (NSTA) and served as a reviewer during the development of Next Generation Science Standards. Dr. Miller holds a doctoral degree from the University of Maryland College Park, a master's degree in school administration and supervision from Bowie State University and a bachelor's degree from Chadron State College.

MICHAEL J. PADILLA, PhD
Professor Emeritus, Eugene P. Moore School of Education, Clemson University, Clemson, South Carolina
Michael J. Padilla taught science in middle and secondary schools, has more than 30 years of experience educating middle-school science teachers, and served as one of the writers of the 1996 U.S. National Science Education Standards. In recent years Mike has focused on teaching science to English Language Learners. His extensive experience as Principal Investigator on numerous National Science Foundation and U.S. Department of Education grants resulted in more than $35 million in funding to improve science education. He served as president of the National Science Teachers Association, the world's largest science teaching organization, in 2005–6.

MICHAEL E. WYSESSION, PhD
Professor of Earth and Planetary Sciences, Washington University, St. Louis, Missouri
Author of more than 100 science and science education publications, Dr. Wysession was awarded the prestigious National Science Foundation Presidential Faculty Fellowship and Packard Foundation Fellowship for his research in geophysics, primarily focused on using seismic tomography to determine the forces driving plate tectonics. Dr. Wysession is also a leader in geoscience literacy and education; he is the chair of the Earth Science Literacy Initiative, the author of several popular video lectures on geology in the *Great Courses* series, and a lead writer of the *Next Generation Science Standards**.

---

*Next Generation Science Standards is a registered trademark of Achieve. Neither Achieve nor the lead states and partners that developed the Next Generation Science Standards were involved in the production of this product, and do not endorse it. NGSS Lead States. 2013. *Next Generation Science Standards: For States, By States.* Washington, DC: The National Academies Press.

REVIEWERS

Program Consultants

Carol Baker
Science Curriculum

Dr. Carol K. Baker is superintendent for Lyons Elementary K-8 School District in Lyons, Illinois. Prior to this, she was Director of Curriculum for Science and Music in Oak Lawn, Illinois. Before this she taught Physics and Earth Science for 18 years. In the recent past, Dr. Baker also wrote assessment questions for ACT (EXPLORE and PLAN), was elected president of the Illinois Science Teachers Association from 2011–2013, and served as a member of the Museum of Science and Industry (Chicago) advisory board. She is a writer of the Next Generation Science Standards. Dr. Baker received her B.S. in Physics and a science teaching certification. She completed her master's of Educational Administration (K-12) and earned her doctorate in Educational Leadership.

Jim Cummins
ELL

Dr. Cummins's research focuses on literacy development in multilingual schools and the role technology plays in learning across the curriculum. *Elevate Science* incorporates research-based principles for integrating language with the teaching of academic content based on Dr. Cummins's work.

Elfrieda Hiebert
Literacy

Dr. Hiebert, a former primary-school teacher, is President and CEO of TextProject, a non-profit aimed at providing open-access resources for instruction of beginning and struggling readers, She is also a research associate at the University of California Santa Cruz. Her research addresses how fluency, vocabulary, and knowledge can be fostered through appropriate texts, and her contributions have been recognized through awards such as the Oscar Causey Award for Outstanding Contributions to Reading Research (Literacy Research Association, 2015), Research to Practice award (American Educational Research Association, 2013), and the William S. Gray Citation of Merit Award for Outstanding Contributions to Reading Research (International Reading Association, 2008).

Content Reviewers

Alex Blom, Ph.D.
Associate Professor
Department Of Physical Sciences
Alverno College
Milwaukee, Wisconsin

Joy Branlund, Ph.D.
Department of Physical Science
Southwestern Illinois College
Granite City, Illinois

Judy Calhoun
Associate Professor
Physical Sciences
Alverno College
Milwaukee, Wisconsin

Stefan Debbert
Associate Professor of Chemistry
Lawrence University
Appleton, Wisconsin

Diane Doser
Professor
Department of Geological Sciences
University of Texas at El Paso
El Paso, Texas

Rick Duhrkopf, Ph.D.
Department of Biology
Baylor University
Waco, Texas

Jennifer Liang
University of Minnesota Duluth
Duluth, Minnesota

Heather Mernitz, Ph.D.
Associate Professor of Physical Sciences
Alverno College
Milwaukee, Wisconsin

Joseph McCullough, Ph.D.
Cabrillo College
Aptos, California

Katie M. Nemeth, Ph.D.
Assistant Professor
College of Science and Engineering
University of Minnesota Duluth
Duluth, Minnesota

Maik Pertermann
Department of Geology
Western Wyoming Community College
Rock Springs, Wyoming

Scott Rochette
Department of the Earth Sciences
The College at Brockport
State University of New York
Brockport, New York

David Schuster
Washington University in St Louis
St. Louis, Missouri

Shannon Stevenson
Department of Biology
University of Minnesota Duluth
Duluth, Minnesota

Paul Stoddard, Ph.D.
Department of Geology and Environmental Geosciences
Northern Illinois University
DeKalb, Illinois

Nancy Taylor
American Public University
Charles Town, West Virginia

Teacher Reviewers

Jennifer Bennett, M.A.
Memorial Middle School
Tampa, Florida

Sonia Blackstone
Lake County Schools
Howey In the Hills, Florida

Teresa Bode
Roosevelt Elementary
Tampa, Florida

Tyler C. Britt, Ed.S.
Curriculum & Instructional Practice Coordinator
Raytown Quality Schools
Raytown, Missouri

A. Colleen Campos
Grandview High School
Aurora, Colorado

Ronald Davis
Riverview Elementary
Riverview, Florida

Coleen Doulk
Challenger School
Spring Hill, Florida

Mary D. Dube
Burnett Middle School
Seffner, Florida

Sandra Galpin
Adams Middle School
Tampa, Florida

Margaret Henry
Lebanon Junior High School
Lebanon, Ohio

Christina Hill
Beth Shields Middle School
Ruskin, Florida

Judy Johnis
Gorden Burnett Middle School
Seffner, Florida

Karen Y. Johnson
Beth Shields Middle School
Ruskin, Florida

Jane Kemp
Lockhart Elementary School
Tampa, Florida

Denise Kuhling
Adams Middle School
Tampa, Florida

Esther Leonard, M.Ed. and L.M.T.
Gifted and talented Implementation Specialist
San Antonio Independent School District
San Antonio, Texas

Kelly Maharaj
Challenger K–8 School of Science and Mathematics
Spring Hill, Florida

Kevin J. Maser, Ed.D.
H. Frank Carey Jr/Sr High School
Franklin Square, New York

Angie L. Matamoros, Ph.D.
ALM Science Consultant
Weston, Florida

Corey Mayle
Brogden Middle School
Durham, North Carolina

Keith McCarthy
George Washington Middle School
Wayne, New Jersey

Yolanda O. Peña
John F. Kennedy Junior High School
West Valley City, Utah

Kathleen M. Poe
Jacksonville Beach Elementary School
Jacksonville Beach, Florida

Wendy Rauld
Monroe Middle School
Tampa, Florida

Anne Rice
Woodland Middle School
Gurnee, Illinois

Bryna Selig
Gaithersburg Middle School
Gaithersburg, Maryland

Pat (Patricia) Shane, Ph.D.
STEM & ELA Education Consultant
Chapel Hill, North Carolina

Diana Shelton
Burnett Middle School
Seffner, Florida

Nakia Sturrup
Jennings Middle School
Seffner, Florida

Melissa Triebwasser
Walden Lake Elementary
Plant City, Florida

Michele Bubley Wiehagen
Science Coach
Miles Elementary School
Tampa, Florida

Pauline Wilcox
Instructional Science Coach
Fox Chapel Middle School
Spring Hill, Florida

Safety Reviewers

Douglas Mandt, M.S.
Science Education Consultant
Edgewood, Washington

Juliana Textley, Ph.D.
Author, NSTA books on school science safety
Adjunct Professor
Lesley University
Cambridge, Massachusetts

TOPIC 1

Cell Processes

MS-LS1-6, MS-LS1-7

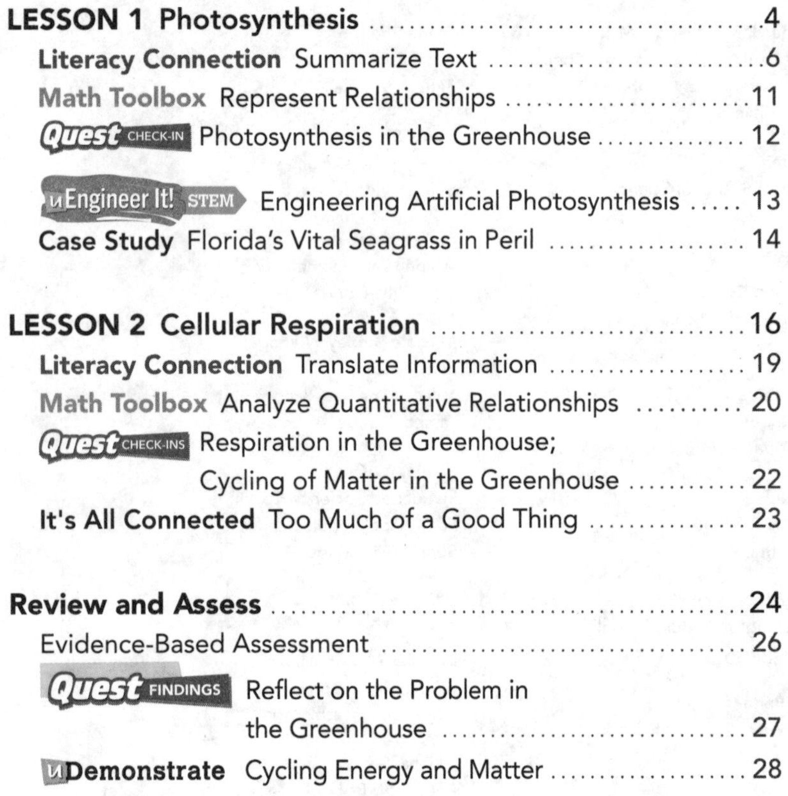

Go to SavvasRealize.com to access your digital course.

VIDEO
- Illustrator

INTERACTIVITY
- The Cell Cycle
- Making Food for Cells
- From Sunlight to Sugar
- Making Energy for Cells
- Energy to Food and Food to Energy

VIRTUAL LAB
- Greenhouse Survival

ASSESSMENT

eTEXT

uConnect Where Does the Energy Come From?

uInvestigate
- Energy From the Sun
- Exhaling Carbon Dioxide

uDemonstrate
Cycling Energy and Matter

TOPIC 2 Ecosystems 32

The Essential Question: How are matter and energy cycled in an ecosystem?

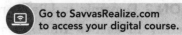

Go to SavvasRealize.com to access your digital course.

VIDEO
- Environmental Engineer

INTERACTIVITY
- There's No Place Like Home
- An Ecological Mystery
- Factors Affecting Growth
- Energy Roles and Flows
- Living Things in an Ecosystem
- A Changing Ecosystem
- Cleaning an Oil Spill
- Cycles of Matter
- Earth's Recyclables

VIRTUAL LAB
- Chesapeake Bay Ecosystem Crisis

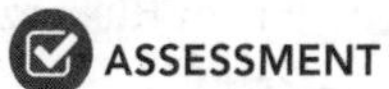

ASSESSMENT

eTEXT

Connect Every Breath You Take

Investigate
- Elbow Room
- Observing Decomposition
- Following Water

Demonstrate
Last Remains

TOPIC 3

Populations, Communities, and Ecosystems 74

MS-LS2-1, MS-LS2-2, MS-LS2-3, MS-LS2-4, MS-LS2-5

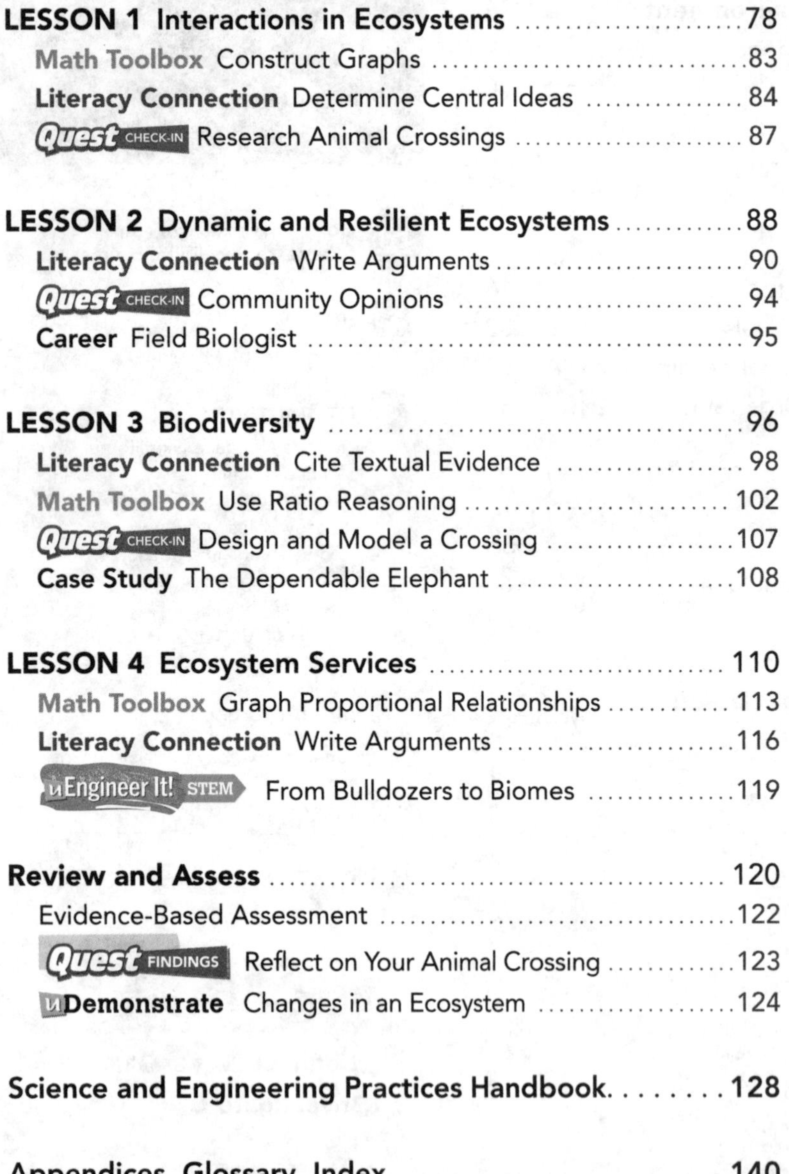

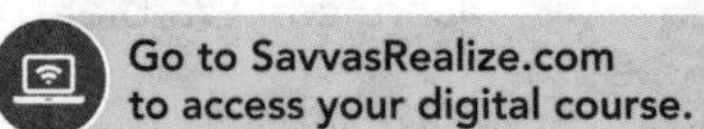

Go to SavvasRealize.com to access your digital course.

VIDEO
- Field Biologist

INTERACTIVITY
- Symbiotic Relationships
- Life on a Reef
- Shared Interactions
- Succession in an Ecosystem
- A Butterfly Mystery
- Biodiversity in the Amazon
- Human Impacts on Biodiversity
- Maintaining Healthy Ecosystems
- Preventing Soil Erosion
- Walk This Way

VIRTUAL LAB
- The Icy World of Polar Bears

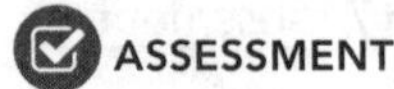

ASSESSMENT

eTEXT

uConnect How Communities Change

uInvestigate
- Competition and Predation
- Primary or Secondary
- Modeling Keystone Species
- Ecosystem Impacts

uDemonstrate
Changes in Ecosystems

Go to SavvasRealize.com to access your digital course.

Elevate Science combines the best science narrative with a robust online program. Throughout the lessons, digital support is presented at point of use to enhance your learning experience.

Online Resources

Savvas Realize™ is your online science class. This digital-learning environment includes:

- Student eTEXT
- Instructor eTEXT
- Project-Based Learning
- Virtual Labs
- Interactivities
- Videos
- Assessments
- Study Tools
- and more!

Digital Features

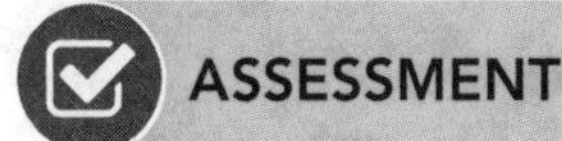

Keep an eye out for these **icons**, which indicate the different ways your textbook is enhanced online.

Digital activities are located throughout the narrative to deepen your understanding of scientific concepts.

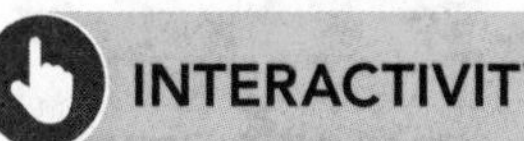

Interpret models of relationships in various ecosystems.

Elevate your thinking!

Elevate Science takes science to a whole new level and lets you take ownership of your learning. Explore science in the world around you. Investigate how things work. Think critically and solve problems! *Elevate Science* helps you think like a scientist, so you're ready for a world of discoveries.

Explore Your World

Explore real-life scenarios with engaging Quests that dig into science topics around the world. You can:

- Solve real-world problems
- Apply skills and knowledge
- Communicate solutions

Quest KICKOFF

What do you think is causing Pleasant Pond to turn green?

In 2016, algal blooms turned bodies of water green and slimy in Florida, Utah, California, and 17 other states. These blooms put people and ecosystems in danger. Scientists, such as limnologists, are working to predict and prevent future algal blooms. In this problem-based Quest activity, you will investigate an algal bloom at a lake and determine its cause. In labs and digital activities, you will apply what you learn in each lesson to help you gather evidence to solve the mystery. With enough evidence, you will be able to identify what you believe is the cause of the algal bloom and present a solution in the Findings activity.

Make Connections

Elevate Science connects science to other subjects and shows you how to better understand the world through:

- Mathematics
- Reading and Writing
- Literacy

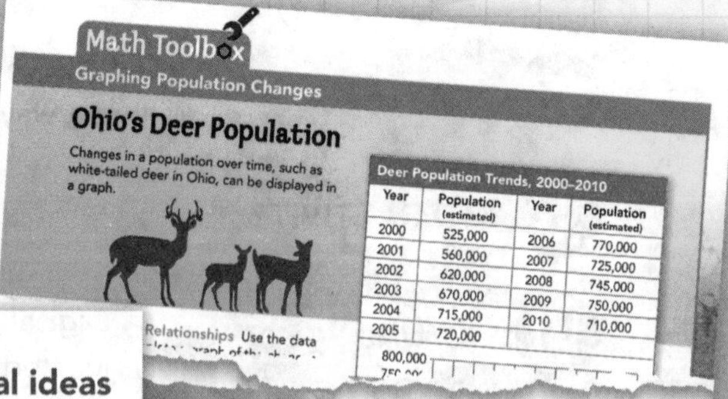

Math Toolbox

Graphing Population Changes

Ohio's Deer Population

Changes in a population over time, such as white-tailed deer in Ohio, can be displayed in a graph.

Deer Population Trends, 2000–2010

Year	Population (estimated)	Year	Population (estimated)
2000	525,000	2006	770,000
2001	560,000	2007	725,000
2002	620,000	2008	745,000
2003	670,000	2009	750,000
2004	715,000	2010	710,000
2005	720,000		

Relationships Use the data

800,000

READING CHECK **Determine Central ideas**
What adaptations might the giraffe have that help it survive in its environment?

Academic Vocabulary

Relate the term *decomposer* to the verb *compose*. What does it mean to compose something?

Build Skills for the Future

- Master the Engineering Design Process
- Apply critical thinking and analytical skills
- Learn about STEM careers

Focus on Inquiry

Case studies put you in the shoes of a scientist to solve real-world mysteries using real data. You will be able to:

- Analyze Data
- Test a hypothesis
- Solve the Case

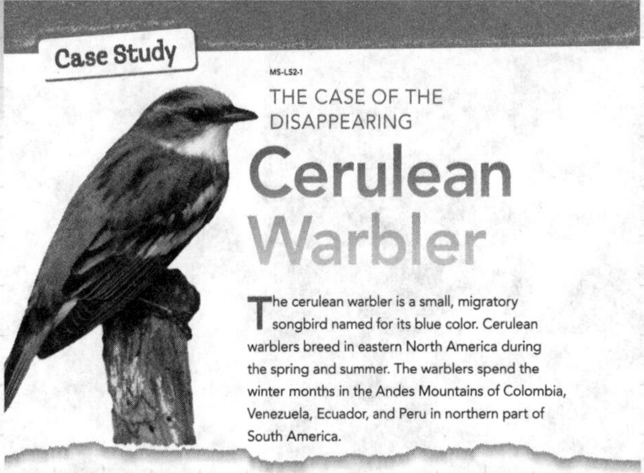

Case Study
MS-LS2-1
THE CASE OF THE DISAPPEARING
Cerulean Warbler
The cerulean warbler is a small, migratory songbird named for its blue color. Cerulean warblers breed in eastern North America during the spring and summer. The warblers spend the winter months in the Andes Mountains of Colombia, Venezuela, Ecuador, and Peru in northern part of South America.

Enter the Lab

Hands-on experiments and virtual labs help you test ideas and show what you know in performance-based assessments. Scaffolded labs include:

- STEM Labs
- Design Your Own
- Open-ended Labs

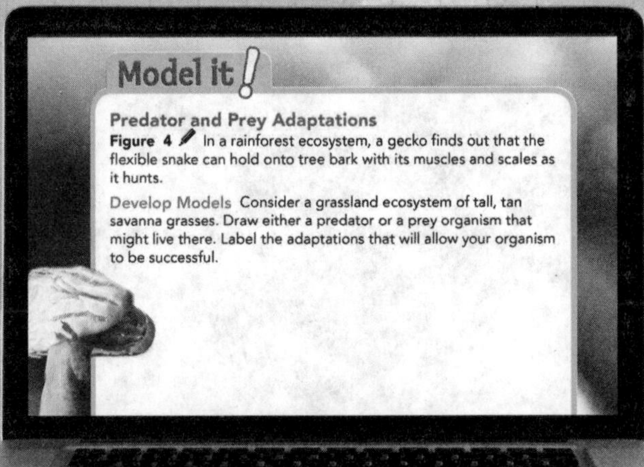

uInvestigate Observe how once-living matter is broken down into smaller components in the process of decomposition.

TOPIC

1

Cell Processes

LESSON 1
Photosynthesis
uInvestigate Lab: Energy From the Sun

LESSON 2
Cellular Respiration
uInvestigate Lab: Modeling Mitosis

uEngineer It! STEM **An Artificial Leaf**

NGSS PERFORMANCE EXPECTATIONS

MS-LS1-6 Construct a scientific explanation based on evidence for the role of photosynthesis in the cycling of matter and flow of energy into and out of organisms.

MS-LS1-7 Develop a model to describe how food is rearranged through chemical reactions forming new molecules that support growth and/or release energy as this matter moves through an organism.

GO ONLINE
to access your digital course

VIDEO

INTERACTIVITY

VIRTUAL LAB

ASSESSMENT

eTEXT

HANDS-ON LABS

Why do baboons eat these strange flowers?

HANDS-ON LAB

uConnect Explore the type of energy used to power a calculator.

The Essential Question How do matter and energy cycle through organisms?

CCC Energy and Matter Baboons in South Africa eat a variety of food, but they are often found enjoying the protea plant and its flowers. The baboons get some of the energy their cells need to live and grow from the protea plants they eat. Where do you think the plants get the energy they need to survive and grow?

....

....

....

....

Quest KICKOFF

What is causing the organisms in the greenhouse to fail?

Phenomenon A horticulturalist working at a botanical garden notices that a greenhouse has been damaged during a storm. The glass shutters that allow air to enter the greenhouse are stuck and won't open. The horticulturalist knows that when a greenhouse can't function properly, there is a negative impact on the plants. In this problem-based Quest activity, you will investigate the factors that may be harming the plants and birds in a neighbor's greenhouse. By applying what you've learned in each lesson to digital activities, you will determine what is going wrong in the greenhouse. Then, in the findings activity, you will develop a plan of action that explains why your recommended steps will solve the problem.

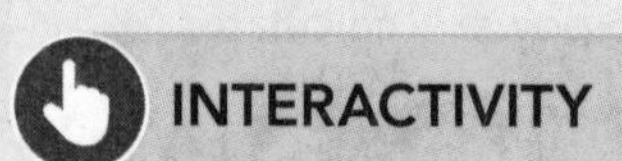

Problem in the Greenhouse

MS-LS1-6, MS-LS1-7

After watching the Quest Kickoff video, which explores vertical farming, consider whether starting a vertical farm at your school would be worthwhile. What are some possible benefits? What are some possible drawbacks? Record your ideas below.

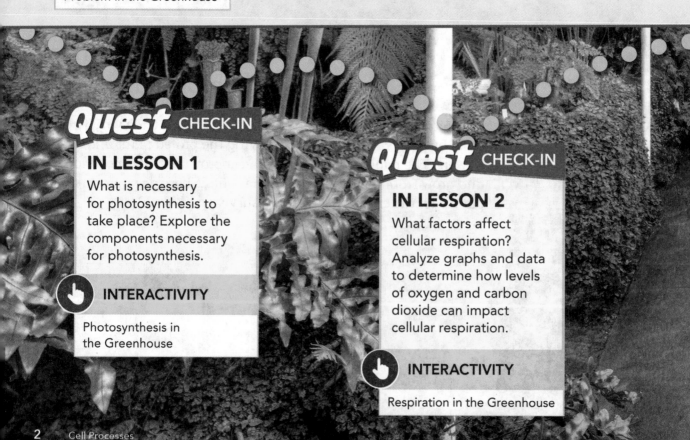

....

....

....

....

....

....

....

Quest CHECK-IN

IN LESSON 1

What is necessary for photosynthesis to take place? Explore the components necessary for photosynthesis.

INTERACTIVITY

Photosynthesis in the Greenhouse

Quest CHECK-IN

IN LESSON 2

What factors affect cellular respiration? Analyze graphs and data to determine how levels of oxygen and carbon dioxide can impact cellular respiration.

INTERACTIVITY

Respiration in the Greenhouse

Greenhouses allow plants to grow even in cold weather.

Quest CHECK-IN

IN LESSON 2

Why is the cycling of matter important in the greenhouse? Model how matter cycles to help determine what might be happening to the plants and birds.

INTERACTIVITY

Cycling of Matter in the Greenhouse

Quest FINDINGS

Complete the Quest!

Create a plan of action, including a diagram, to identify the steps your neighbor can take to solve the greenhouse problem.

INTERACTIVITY

Reflect on the Problem in the Greenhouse

uConnect Lab

Where Does the Energy Come From?

How can **design a procedure** to help you determine which type of energy makes something work?

Background

Phenomenon You get the energy you need to walk, run, and think from the food you eat. Energy, however, comes in many different forms. In this activity, you will determine the type of energy used to power a calculator.

(per group)

- solar-powered calculator

Design a Procedure

☐ **1. SEP Plan an Investigation** Describe how you plan to investigate which kind of energy powers the calculator.

....

....

....

....

....

....

....

☐ **2.** Show your plan to your teacher for approval, and then begin your investigation. Record your observations.

Observations

uConnect Go online for a downloadable worksheet of this lab.

Analyze and Conclude

1. **CCC Patterns** Did you observe any changes in the function of your calculator as you worked through your investigation?

2. **SEP Construct an Explanation** Based on your observations, what can you infer about the energy that powers the calculator? Explain using evidence from your investigation.

LESSON

1 Photosynthesis

Guiding Questions

- How do plants and other organisms use photosynthesis to make food?
- What are the roles of light, carbon dioxide, water, and chlorophyll in photosynthesis?
- What role does photosynthesis play in cycling materials and energy through ecosystems?

Connections

Literacy Summarize Text

Math Represent Relationships

MS-LS1-6, MS-LS1-7, MS-LS2-3

HANDS-ON LAB

uInvestigate Explore why one stage of photosynthesis can take place in the dark.

Vocabulary

photosynthesis
autotroph
heterotroph
chlorophyll

Academic Vocabulary

equation

Connect It!

In the boxes, write the direct source of energy for each organism.

SEP Evaluate Evidence Which of the organisms shown does not eat another organism for food?

....

CCC Cause and Effect What do you think would happen to each species if the water became too cloudy for sunlight to penetrate?

....

....

....

....

Living Things and Energy

Off the Pacific coast, from Alaska to California, sea urchins graze on kelp beds under water. A sea otter begins the hunt for lunch as they always have and hopefully always will. The otter will take urchins off kelp to eat them at the surface.

Both the sea urchins and the otter in **Figure 1** use the food they eat to obtain energy. Every living thing needs energy. All the cells in every organism need energy to carry out their functions, such as making proteins and transporting substances into and out of the cell. Energy used by living things comes from their environment, similar to the raw materials cells use to function. Meat from the sea urchin provides the otter's cells with energy, while kelp provides energy for the cells of the sea urchin. Where does the energy in the kelp come from? Plants, algae, phytoplankton (floating algae), and some microorganisms including bacteria, obtain their energy differently. These organisms use the energy from sunlight to make their own food.

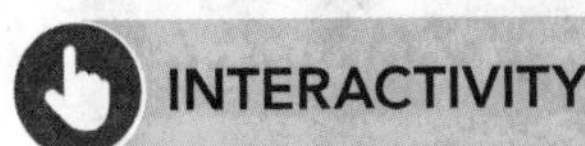

Identify what items are considered food.

Energy for Life

Figure 1 All living things—such as California sea otters, sea urchins, and kelp—need energy to survive.

CCC Cause and Effect What would likely happen to the kelp if the otters died off?

....

....

....

....

....

kelp

sea urchins

otter

Literacy Connection

Summarize Text In your own words, summarize the main idea of the passage on this page.

....

....

....

....

....

....

....

....

....

Energy From the Sun Cells capture energy in sunlight and use it to make food in a process called **photosynthesis.** The term *photosynthesis* comes from the Greek words *photos*, which means "light," and *syntithenai*, which means "putting together." Plants and other photosynthetic organisms link molecules together into useful forms using photosynthesis.

Nearly all living things obtain energy directly or indirectly from the sun's energy. This energy is captured from the sunlight during photosynthesis. In **Figure 2,** the leaf obtains energy directly from sunlight because plants use sunlight to make their own food during photosynthesis. When you eat an apple, you get energy from the sun that has been stored in the apple. You get the sun's energy indirectly from the energy that the apple tree gained through photosynthesis.

An Energy Chain

Figure 2 The energy of sunlight passes from one organism to another.

CCC Energy and Matter ✏ Draw arrows showing the flow of energy from the sun.

Making and Obtaining Food Plants make their own food through the process of photosynthesis. **Autotrophs**, or producers, are able to create their own food in the form of glucose, an energy-giving sugar. Plants and algae, as well as some bacteria, are autotrophs. An organism that cannot make its own food, such as the sea urchin or otter, is a consumer, or a **heterotroph.** Many heterotrophs, like the fox in **Figure 3**, obtain food by eating other organisms. Some heterotrophs, such as fungi, absorb their food from other organisms.

Reflect How is sunlight important to plant growth? In your science notebook, list some questions you have about the effects of sunlight on growing plants.

Summarize Text What is the difference between heterotrophs and autotrophs?

....

....

....

Model It!

Trace Energy to the Source

Figure 3 A gray fox captures and eats prey like rabbits and hares that depend on plants for food.

CCC Systems and System Models Draw a diagram that tracks how the sun's energy gets to the fox. In your diagram, label each organism as a heterotroph or an autotroph.

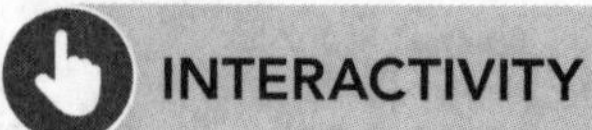

INTERACTIVITY

Describe the cycling of matter and energy that occurs during photosynthesis.

HANDS-ON LAB

Investigate Explore why one stage of photosynthesis can take place in the dark.

Student Discourse
After reading about Stage 1 of photosynthesis and completing Figure 4, form a small group with classmates. Write down two questions about Stage 1. Then each group member should offer a question for the group to discuss.

Photosynthesis

Photosynthesis is a chemical reaction in plants that uses light energy to convert certain types of matter into another they can use as food. It takes place mostly in chloroplasts, as shown in **Figure 4.** When plants use the sun's energy to convert carbon dioxide from the atmosphere and water into sugar, oxygen is produced. Because photosynthesis is a chemical reaction, several different factors affect the rate of chemical change. The availability of sunlight, water, and carbon dioxide are all factors required for photosynthesis.

Stage 1: Trapping the Sun's Energy

Chloroplasts, the green organelles in plant cells, use chlorophyll to absorb sunlight during the first stage of photosynthesis. The green color comes from pigments, which are colored chemical compounds that absorb light. The green photosynthetic pigment found in the chloroplasts of plants, algae, and some bacteria is **chlorophyll**.

Picture solar cells in a solar-powered calculator. Chlorophyll functions in a similar way. Chlorophyll captures light energy that the chloroplast uses to create oxygen gas and sugar (**Figure 4**).

During Stage 1, sunlight splits water molecules in the chloroplasts into hydrogen and oxygen. The hydrogen combines with other atoms during Stage 2 and the oxygen is released into the environment as a waste product. A product is the substance formed after a reaction takes place. Some oxygen gas exits a leaf through openings on the leaf's underside. Almost all the oxygen in Earth's atmosphere is produced by living things through the process of photosynthesis.

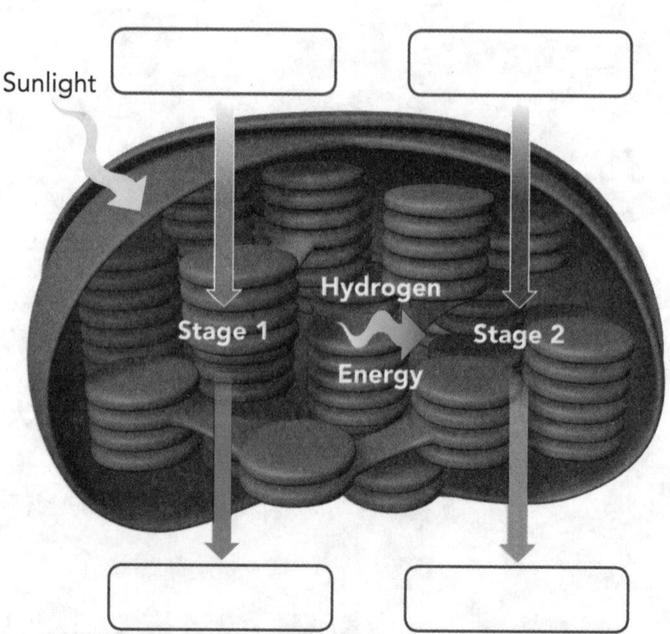

Photosynthesis: Stages 1 and 2

Figure 4 Photosynthesis takes place in the chloroplasts. Specialized structures in each chloroplast contain chlorophyll.

CCC Energy and Matter
Add labels to the arrows in the diagram to indicate whether water, carbon dioxide, sugar, or oxygen is entering or leaving.

Stage 2: Making Food In Stage 2 of photosynthesis, cells produce sugar. Sugars are carbon-based organic molecules that are useful for storing chemical energy or for building larger molecules. Glucose, which has the chemical formula $C_6H_{12}O_6$, is one of the most important sugars produced in photosynthesis. The energy stored in the chemical bonds of glucose allows cells to carry out vital functions.

The production of glucose is shown in **Figure 5.** Hydrogen (H) that came from splitting water molecules in Stage 1 is one reactant, the substance undergoing a change during a reaction. The other reactant is carbon dioxide (CO_2) from the air. Carbon dioxide enters the plant through the small openings on the underside of each leaf and moves into the chloroplasts. Powered by the energy captured in Stage 1, hydrogen and carbon dioxide undergo a series of reactions to produce glucose.

READING CHECK Integrate with Visuals
On the picture, write R in the circles for the two raw materials, or reactants, of photosynthesis, E in the circle for the energy source, and P in the circles of the two products.

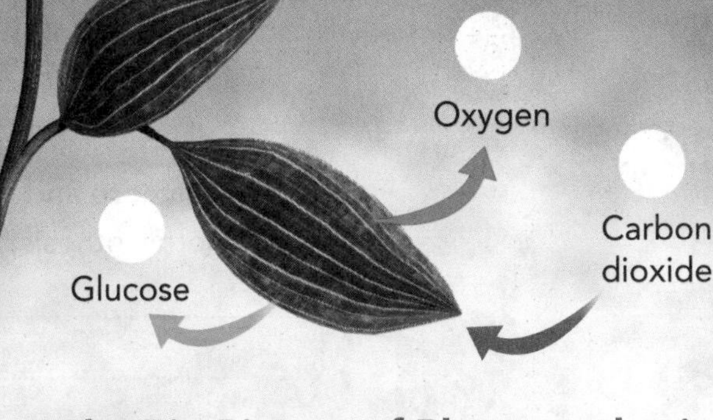

The Big Picture of Photosynthesis
Figure 5 This view of photosynthesis is from outside the plant. Plant cells also break down glucose to release the energy they need to grow and reproduce.

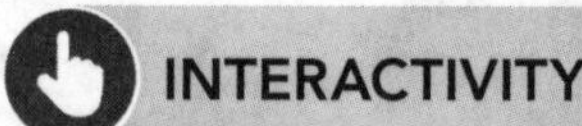

Determine what factors influence photosynthesis in modern and ancient plants.

Academic Vocabulary

How is a chemical equation similar to a mathematical equation, and how do they model a natural phenomenon?

Expressing Photosynthesis

The events of photosynthesis that lead to the production of glucose can be expressed as the following chemical **equation**:

$$\underset{\text{light energy}}{} + \underset{\text{carbon dioxide}}{6\,CO_2} + \underset{\text{water}}{6\,H_2O} \longrightarrow \underset{\text{glucose}}{C_6H_{12}O_6} + \underset{\text{oxygen}}{6\,O_2}$$

Notice that six molecules of carbon dioxide and six molecules of water are in the equation to the left of the arrow. These compounds are raw materials, or reactants. One molecule of glucose and six molecules of oxygen are on the right side of the arrow. These compounds are products. An arrow, which means "yields," points from the reactants to the products. Energy is not a reactant, but it is written on the left side of the equation to show that it is used in the reaction. There are the same number of atoms of each element on both sides of the equation—no matter is gained or lost.

Plant cells use some glucose produced in photosynthesis for food. The cells break down sugar molecules in a process called cellular respiration. The energy released from glucose can be used to carry out a plant's functions (**Figure 6**), such as growth. Other glucose molecules are stored for later use. When you eat food from plant roots, such as potatoes or carrots, you are eating the plant's stored energy.

READING CHECK **Determine Central Ideas** What happens to glucose and oxygen that is produced by plants during photosynthesis?

Photosynthesis Is the Key

Figure 6 Green plants use the sugars produced in photosynthesis in many ways.

SEP Communicate Information Label the leaves, roots, and seeds in the diagram. Then fill in the boxes with some of the ways plants use the products of photosynthesis.

Importance of Plant Cells

Plant cells were the first cells to be seen with a microscope. Because plant cell walls are like rigid boxes, plant cells do not burst when placed in an aquatic environment. The ability to store water is one reason that marshes are so important (**Figure 7**). During storms with heavy rainfall, such as hurricanes, marsh plants soak up water. For this reason, marshland is considered a natural flood control.

Plants and algae that live in water absorb about one sixth of all the sun's energy that falls on Earth. Ocean plants play an essential role in recycling oxygen. In fact, 85 percent of the oxygen in Earth's atmosphere comes from ocean plants. They perform photosynthesis much like land plants. They collect the sun's energy and take in carbon dioxide. They always have water. They use these reactants to produce food (energy) for themselves and to release oxygen into the water for use by other organisms.

Marsh Plants

Figure 7 The marsh in the Vic Fazio Yolo Wildlife Area is managed to help protect Sacramento, California, from flooding. It also provides prime habitat to nearly 200 species of birds and other wetland wildlife.

SEP Construct Explanations How do marshes control flooding?

....

....

All in the Balance

The photosynthesis equation states that 6 CO_2 and 6 H_2O molecules combine to form 1 $C_6H_{12}O_6$ molecule and 6 O_2 molecules. For every 6 carbon dioxide molecules, the reaction produces 1 glucose molecule.

1. **SEP Use Mathematics** Write an equation using two variables to model how many glucose molecules are produced by 6 CO_2 molecules. Use *x* for the number of glucose molecules and *y* for the number of CO_2 molecules.

   ....

2. **CCC Scale, Proportion, and Quantity** Calculate how many glucose molecules are produced by 6, 12, 18, and 24 CO_2 molecules. Plot these points on the graph. What is the relationship between the two variables?

   ....

   ....

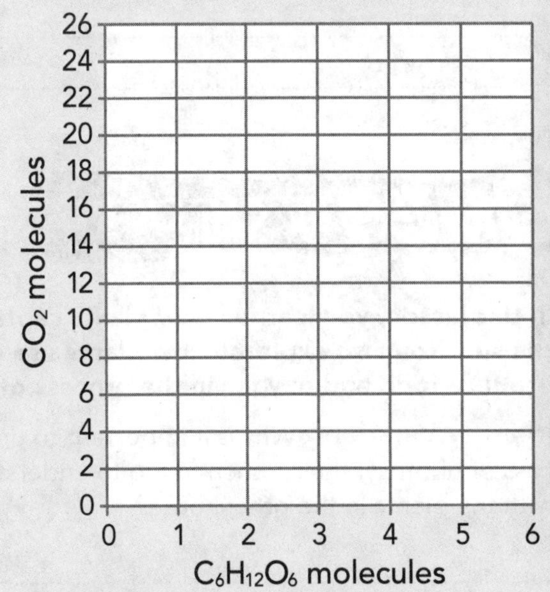

LESSON 1 Check

MS-LS1-6, MS-LS1-7, MS-LS2-3

1. **CCC Systems** Where does a plant get the energy necessary to drive the chemical reaction in photosynthesis?

2. **SEP Cite Evidence** How do you know an organism is a heterotroph? Name three heterotrophs.

3. **Identify** What are the raw materials, or reactants, for Stage 2 of photosynthesis, and where do these materials come from?

4. **CCC Energy and Matter** How does chlorophyll help the functioning of chloroplasts?

5. **CCC Energy and Matter** What are the roles of light, carbon dioxide, and water molecules in the production of food and oxygen in photosynthesis?

6. **SEP Develop Models** Draw the same plant on a sunny day and a cloudy day. In your model, show on which day it would likely produce less oxygen. In your labels, show which part of the chemical reaction of photosynthesis would be affected. (Smaller versions of **Figure 5** might be good starting points.)

Quest CHECK-IN

In this lesson, you learned how plants capture energy from the sun. You also explored how plants use carbon dioxide to produce food and oxygen in the process of photosynthesis.

Identify Variables Why is it important to understand the process of photosynthesis when trying to understand what is wrong with the plants in the greenhouse?

INTERACTIVITY

Photosynthesis in the Greenhouse

Go online to explore how temperature, carbon dioxide levels, and light intensity can affect a plant's ability to carry out photosynthesis.

MS-LS1-6

Engineering Artificial PHOTOSYNTHESIS

Examine how the different parts of an artificial leaf work.

How do you make photosynthesis more efficient? You engineer it!

The Challenge: To create a more efficient form of photosynthesis.

Phenomenon Photosynthesis is an important process for all life on Earth. However, it isn't very efficient. Only 1 percent of the sunlight that hits a leaf is used during the process of photosynthesis.

Scientists at the Joint Center for Artificial Photosynthesis (JCAP) in California hope to engineer ways of improving that efficiency. Founded in 2010 by the U.S. Department of Energy, the center has one main goal: to find a way to produce fossil fuel alternatives using just sunlight, water, and carbon dioxide. The center is led by a team of scientists and researchers at the California Institute of Technology in partnership with the Lawrence Berkeley National Laboratory. JCAP's facilities have state-of-the-art tools and technologies at its disposal for scientists to conduct investigations and experiments of just about any kind as they relate to photosynthesis.

JCAP scientists are developing solar fuel generators (shown here) that mimic the process of photosynthesis with greater efficiency.

In his 2011 State of the Union address to Congress, President Obama singled out the work of JCAP researchers: "We're issuing a challenge. We're telling America's scientists and engineers that if they assemble teams of the best minds in their fields, and focus on the hardest problems in clean energy, we'll fund the Apollo projects of our time. At the California Institute of Technology, they're developing a way to turn sunlight and water into fuel for our cars."

DESIGN CHALLENGE
Can you build a model of a tree that uses artificial leaves and artificial photosynthesis? Go to the Engineering Design Notebook to find out!

Case Study

MS-LS1-6

Florida's Vital Seagrass in Peril

In 2014, disaster struck the seagrass ecosystems along Florida's shores. These habitats provide food and shelter to fish and other animals such as crabs, shrimp, oysters, and starfish. The area serves as a nursery, protecting eggs and juveniles.

The seagrass beds are a popular place for recreational fishing. They also support commercial fishing and shellfish harvests that bring billions of dollars a year into the Florida economy.

River flow normally supplies fresh water to maintain a salt level that permits seagrass growth. Drought increases salt concentrations to levels the seagrass can't tolerate.

Healthy seagrass is abundant and green.

Seagrass in water with high salinity (salt) levels fails to thrive.

Impact of the Die-off

As the seagrass ecosystem collapsed, oxygen levels in the water decreased. The fish and invertebrates had to move or die. The nurseries protecting young fish could no longer provide food and protection. As the populations fell, this also affected commercial and recreational fishing.

The seagrass ecosystem was already under stress, especially from human impact. Pollution, diseases, excessive nutrients from farm runoff, and damage from boat propellers all harmed the ecosystem.

While droughts may not be preventable, there are actions people can take to protect this habitat. Water conservation ensures that freshwater keeps flowing into the beds. Limiting fertilizer use can minimize nutrient runoff. Restricting motorboat access can keep the seagrasses intact. All of the these steps protect a vital resource that protects so many others.

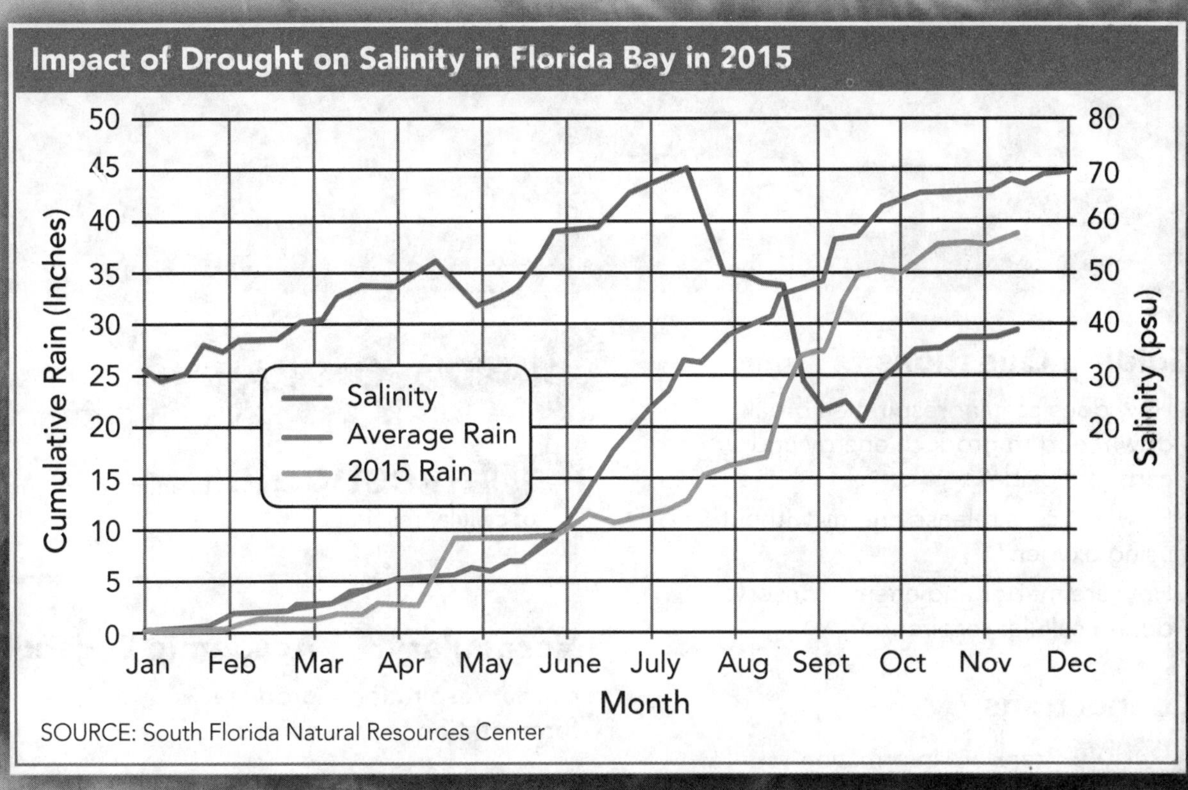

Use the graph and the information on the previous page to answer the following questions.

1. **Patterns** What is the relationship between rainfall, salinity, and time of year?

2. **Predict** What do you think would happen to the seagrass if a persistent drought continued for several years? Explain.

3. **Construct Explanations** How would reduced levels of light affect the seagrasses' rates of photosynthesis?

4. **Connect to Society** How can people get involved to try to save the essential seagrass beds?

LESSON 2

Cellular Respiration

Guiding Questions

- How does cellular respiration break down food to produce energy and carbon dioxide?
- How can cells release energy without using oxygen?
- How are matter and energy conserved during cellular respiration?

Connections

Literacy Translate Information

Math Analyze Quantitative Relationships

MS-LS1-6, MS-LS1-7

HANDS-ON LAB

uInvestigate Examine a product of cellular respiration.

Vocabulary

cellular respiration
fermentation

Academic Vocabulary

produce
source

Connect It!

Draw arrows on Figure 1 to show the flow of energy from the food into the bikers, and then out into the environment as heat and motion.

SEP Use Mathematics

Sketch on the graph to show how the bikers' energy level may change over time as they start biking, stop for a snack, start biking again, and finish their ride.

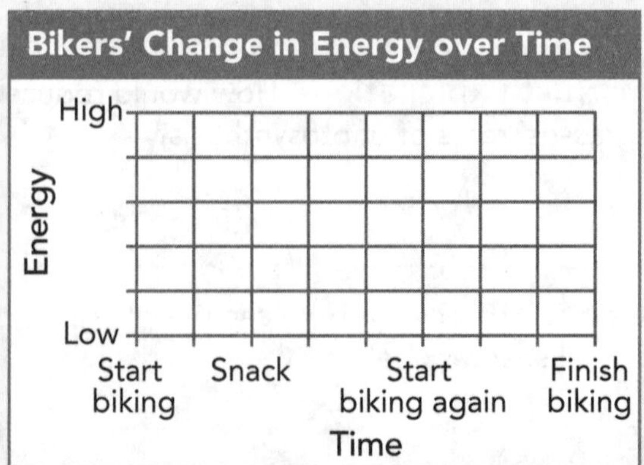

Energy and Cellular Respiration

You and your friend have been biking all morning. The steepest part of the road is ahead. You'll need a lot of energy to get to the top! The food shown in **Figure 1** will provide some of that energy.

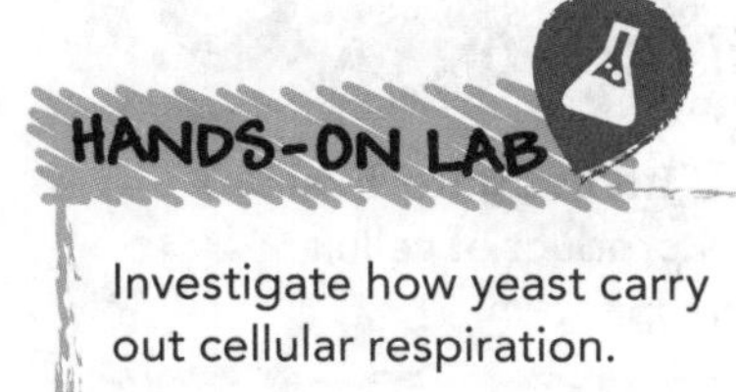

Investigate how yeast carry out cellular respiration.

Plants and animals break down food into small, usable molecules, such as glucose. Energy stored in these molecules is released so the cell can carry out functions. **Cellular respiration** is the process in which oxygen and glucose undergo a complex series of chemical reactions inside cells, releasing energy. All living things need energy. Therefore, all living things carry out cellular respiration.

Using Energy A hot water heater stores hot water. To wash your hands, you turn on the faucet and draw out the needed hot water. Your body stores and uses energy in a similar way. When you eat, you add to your body's energy account by storing glucose, fat, and other substances. When cells need energy, they "draw it out" by breaking down the energy-rich compounds through cellular respiration.

Respiration People often use the word *respiration* when they mean *breathing*, the physical movement of air in and out of your lungs. In the study of the life sciences, however, respiration and breathing are not interchangeable. Breathing brings oxygen into your lungs. Cells use oxygen in cellular respiration. Exhaling removes the waste products of that process from your body.

Food for Energy

Figure 1 Biking takes a lot of energy! Your body uses cellular respiration to get energy from the food you eat, such as trail mix.

Investigate Examine a product of cellular respiration.

Cellular Respiration Process

Cellular Respiration Process Like photosynthesis, cellular respiration is a two-stage process. **Figure 2** shows both stages of cellular respiration. Stage 1 occurs in the cell's cytoplasm, where glucose is broken down into smaller molecules. Oxygen is not involved in this stage, and only a small amount of energy is released. Stage 2 occurs in a mitochondrion and uses oxygen. The smaller molecules produced in Stage 1 are broken down even more. Stage 2 releases a great deal of energy that the cell can use for all its activities.

Academic Vocabulary

How can the terms *produce* and *source* be used to describe a nation's economy?

....

....

....

....

Cellular Respiration Equation The raw materials for cellular respiration are glucose and oxygen. Heterotrophs get glucose from consuming food. Autotrophs carry out photosynthesis to **produce** their own glucose. Air is the **source** of oxygen. The products of cellular respiration are carbon dioxide and water. Although respiration occurs in a series of complex steps, the overall process can be summarized in the equation:

$$\underset{\text{glucose}}{C_6H_{12}O_6} + \underset{\text{oxygen}}{6\,O_2} \longrightarrow \underset{\text{carbon dioxide}}{6\,CO_2} + \underset{\text{water}}{6\,H_2O} + \text{energy}$$

Releasing Energy

Figure 2 Cellular respiration takes place in two stages.

Integrate Information Fill in the missing terms in the spaces provided.

Stage 1 In the cytoplasm, ... is broken down into smaller molecules, releasing a small amount of ....

Stage 2 In the ...., the smaller molecules react, producing ...., water, and large amounts of ....

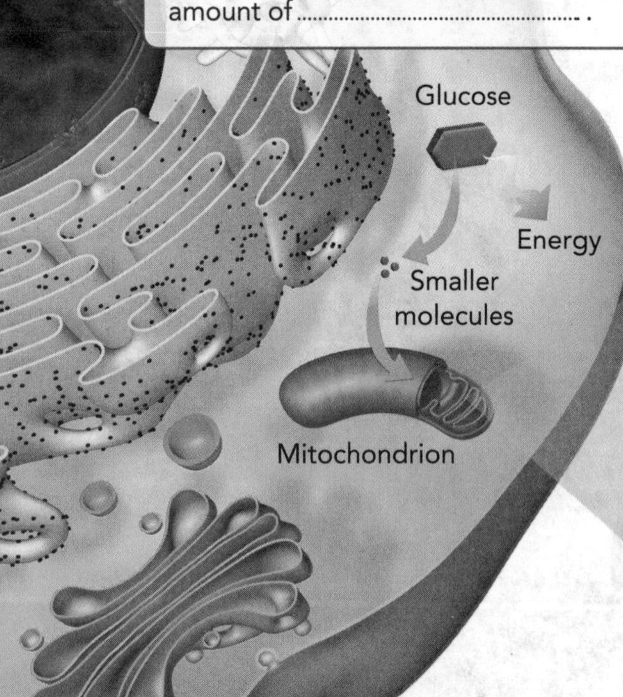

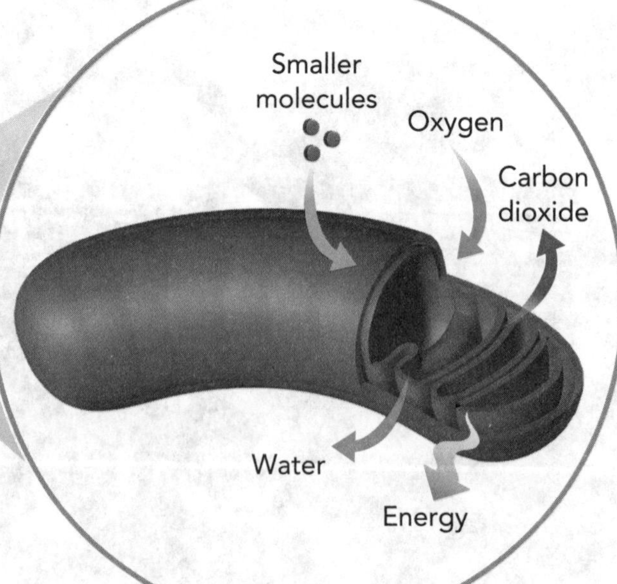

Role of Mitochondria It may be a small organelle, but the mitochondrion (plural, mitochondria) is well known as the cell's powerhouse. The function of the mitochondrion is to create large amounts of energy. In **Figure 2**, notice how the mitochondrion is structured. The folds inside the organelle create more surface area. Chemical reactions occur on these folds. Because of this increased surface area, many more chemical reactions can occur. In turn, more energy is created. Cells that need a great deal of energy may have thousands of mitochondria. If a cell needs more energy to survive, it can create more mitochondria.

Not all organisms use glucose and oxygen to carry out cellular respiration. Some organisms rely on a type of cellular respiration that uses fructose instead of glucose to create energy. For this chemical reaction, they do not need oxygen to break down the fructose.

READING CHECK **Determine Conclusions** Think about the job of the mitochondria. Which cells in your body would you expect to have the most mitochondria? Explain your reasoning.

....

....

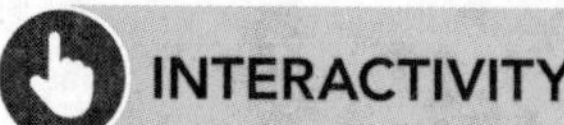

Explore what happens when the body breaks down glucose.

Literacy Connection

Translate Information In **Figure 2**, circle the folds in the mitochondrion that increase the organelle's surface area.

Reflect "Respiration" can also refer to breathing. Is some sort of "breathing" required for cellular respiration to occur? Do plants "breathe"?

Model It!

SEP Develop Models Create a model of a mitochondrion showing its roles during cellular respiration. Show both the activities that occur there and all the reactants it uses and and products released there.

Related Processes

Figure 3 Carbon dioxide and oxygen cycle through cellular respiration and photosynthesis.

1. CCC Structure and Function ✎ Label the diagram to complete each of the processes.
2. Connect to the Environment Why do you think it is important for us to decrease the release of carbon dioxide gas even though autotrophs take it in during photosynthesis?

....

....

....

....

....

....

....

Comparing Two Energy Processes If you think the equation for cellular respiration is the opposite of the one for photosynthesis, you're right! Photosynthesis and cellular respiration can be thought of as opposite processes. The two processes form a cycle, keeping the levels of oxygen and carbon dioxide molecules relatively stable in Earth's atmosphere. As shown in **Figure 3**, living things cycle both gases repeatedly. The energy released through cellular respiration is used or lost as heat. Matter and energy is neither created or destroyed in this cycle.

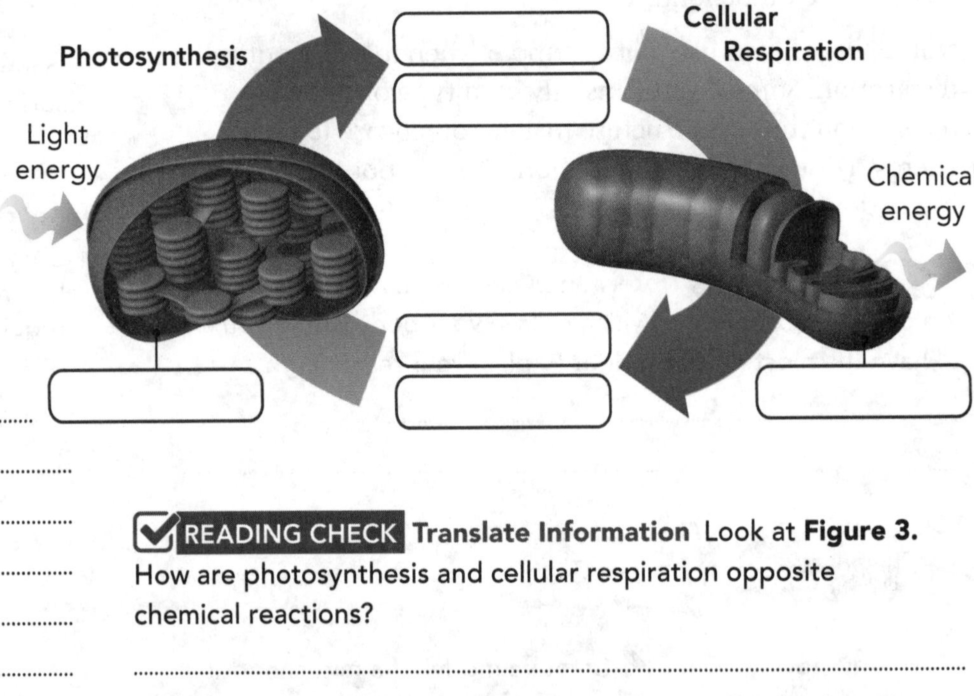

READING CHECK **Translate Information** Look at **Figure 3.** How are photosynthesis and cellular respiration opposite chemical reactions?

....

....

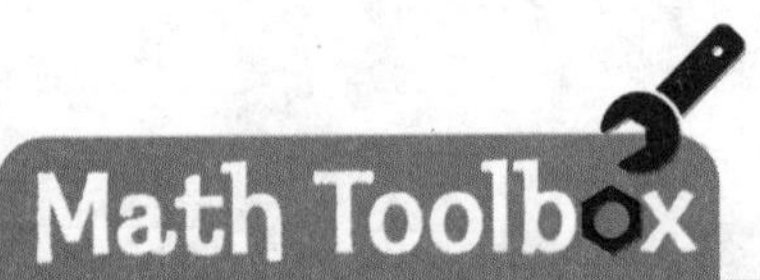

Math Toolbox

Conservation of Matter in the Balance

In a chemical reaction, matter is neither created nor destroyed. For this reason, every chemical equation is balanced. You will find the same number of each kind of atom on both sides of the equation for cellular respiration.

SEP Use Mathematics ✎ Do the math to prove that the equation for cellular respiration is balanced for oxygen and carbon. Review the equation for cellular respiration below and complete the table.

$$C_6H_{12}O_6 + 6\ O_2 \longrightarrow 6\ CO_2 + 6\ H_2O$$

	Atoms on left side	Atoms on right side	Balanced? Yes or No
Oxygen (O)			
Carbon (C)			

Fermentation

Yeast, bacteria, and your own muscle cells can release energy from food without oxygen. The release of energy from food without using oxygen is called **fermentation**. Fermentation is very useful in environments with limited oxygen, such as in the intestines. However, fermentation releases much less energy than cellular respiration with oxygen.

Alcoholic Fermentation When you eat a slice of bread, you are eating a product of fermentation. Alcoholic fermentation takes place in live yeast cells—unicellular fungi—and in other single-celled organisms. This type of fermentation produces alcohol, carbon dioxide, and a small amount of energy. Bakers use these products of fermentation. Carbon dioxide creates gas pockets in bread dough. This causes the dough to rise.

Lactic Acid Fermentation Have you ever run as fast and hard as you could, like the sprinter in **Figure 4**? Although you started to breathe faster, your muscle cells used up oxygen faster than it could be replaced. Without enough oxygen, fermentation takes place. Your body supplies energy to your muscle cells by breaking down glucose without using oxygen. A compound called lactic acid is a product of fermentation in muscles. One popular misconception is that lactic acid "builds up in the muscles" and causes "muscle burn" as well as any lingering soreness. However, lactic acid actually fuels your muscles and goes away shortly after the workout. During exercise and intense physical activity, your body needs ATP—a substance the cells use as an energy source to meet high demands for energy. When the cells use ATP, it produces a proton. As protons pile up, the immediate area becomes acidic. The nerves near the muscles sense this acidity as muscle burn. But that sensation has nothing to do with lactic acid.

READING CHECK **Determine Central Ideas** How does fermentation that causes dough to rise differ from fermentation in muscles?

....

....

Running Out of Oxygen

Figure 4 Your breathing and blood circulation can supply enough oxygen for cellular respiration when you exercise gently. During a sprint, your cells run low on oxygen and switch to lactic acid fermentation for energy.

SEP Evaluate Evidence For each activity, label the source of energy for the muscle cells. Is it oxygen or lactic acid?

LESSON 2 Check

MS-LS1-6, MS-LS1-7

1. **CCC Construct Explanations** Do plants and animals both use cellular respiration? Explain.

2. **SEP Develop Models** In the space below, sketch and label a diagram showing the relationship between photosynthesis and cellular respiration.

3. **Communicate** Where does each stage of cellular respiration take place in the cell?

4. **Apply Concepts** How do heterotrophs get energy? Explain.

5. **SEP Engage in an Argument** A classmate states that both energy and matter can be created during photosynthesis and cellular respiration. Use the chemical equations for the processes to respond to your classmate.

Quest CHECK-INS

In this lesson, you learned about the process of cellular respiration, in which the cells of an organism use sugar and oxygen to produce energy and carbon dioxide.

Evaluate Why is it important to consider the process of cellular respiration when determining what is going wrong in the greenhouse?

INTERACTIVITIES

Respiration in the Greenhouse; Cycling of Matter in the Greenhouse

Go online to learn about the factors that affect the process of cellular respiration. Consider how these factors might explain why the greenhouse is failing. Then analyze the data from the sensors in the greenhouse. Make some generalizations about the data to help you begin developing your action plan.

MS-LS1-7

Too Much of a Good Thing

Almost everyone loves sweets. After all, they taste really good. But sugary foods have negative effects on our health. The sugar we eat is broken down by our cells for energy. Under normal circumstances, cells break down all the sugar they receive and produce enough energy. However, what happens when cells get too much sugar?

Our bodies need one important sugar to survive—glucose—and it's serious fuel for your brain, too. So how can sugar hurt us? The problem is that we do not limit our sugar intake to what occurs naturally in fruits and vegetables. Most of the sugar we eat is sugar that gets added to foods and beverages like sodas and energy drinks. And there is way too much of it.

One health consequence of eating too much sugar is obesity, which puts people at a higher risk for diabetes or even a heart attack. Another consequence is "brain decay." Some studies show that mental decline is one outcome for people who develop diabetes. Then there is cancer. Other studies show that people who consume high levels of sugar have a much higher risk of getting cancer.

CONNECT TO YOU

Should schools sell candy and soft drinks to students?

The average teen consumes 22–34 teaspoons of added sugars each day. This 12-ounce serving of soda has about 10 teaspoons of sugar. The recommended amount of added sugars for teens each day is no more than 9 teaspoons.

☑ TOPIC 1 Review and Assess

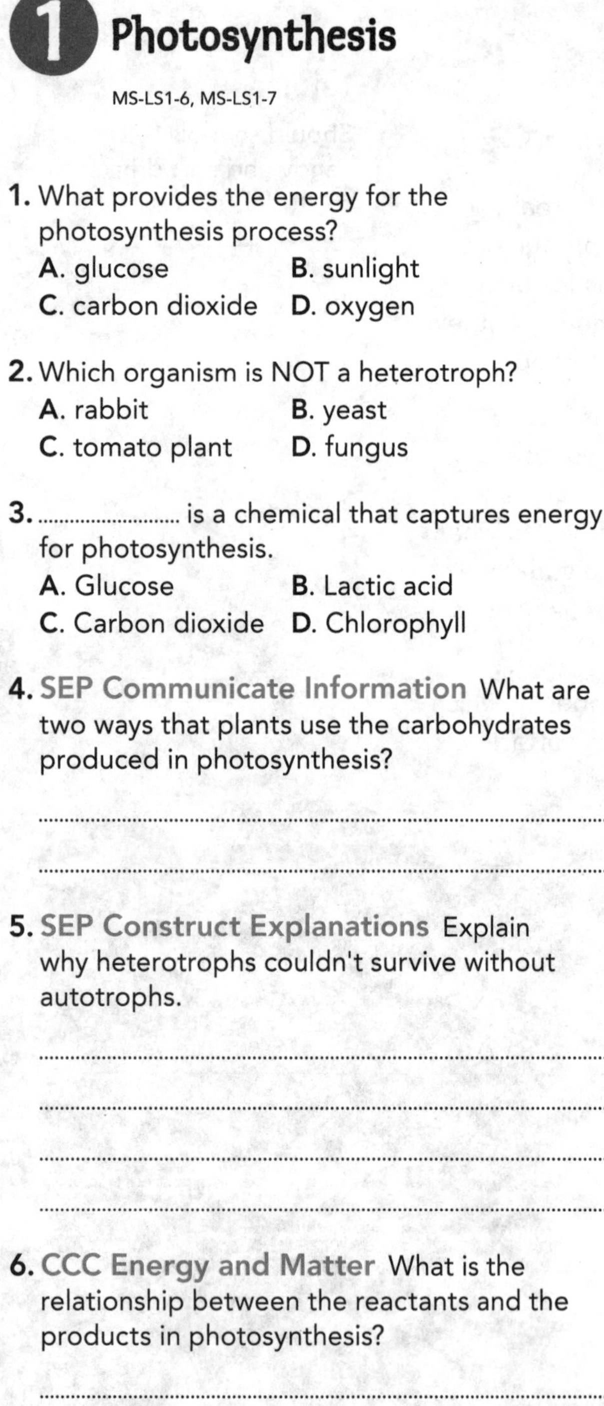

1 Photosynthesis

MS-LS1-6, MS-LS1-7

1. What provides the energy for the photosynthesis process?
   A. glucose B. sunlight
   C. carbon dioxide D. oxygen

2. Which organism is NOT a heterotroph?
   A. rabbit B. yeast
   C. tomato plant D. fungus

3. .... is a chemical that captures energy for photosynthesis.
   A. Glucose B. Lactic acid
   C. Carbon dioxide D. Chlorophyll

4. **SEP Communicate Information** What are two ways that plants use the carbohydrates produced in photosynthesis?

5. **SEP Construct Explanations** Explain why heterotrophs couldn't survive without autotrophs.

6. **CCC Energy and Matter** What is the relationship between the reactants and the products in photosynthesis?

7. **SEP Construct Explanations** The concentration of carbon dioxide in the atmosphere has been gradually increasing for many years. How might this increase affect photosynthesis?

8. **SEP Develop Models** ✏ Draw and label a diagram to describe Stage 1 of photosynthesis. What is produced? What is released?

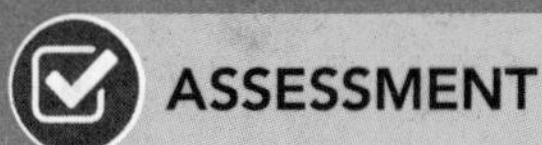

Evaluate your understanding by taking a Topic Test.

2 Cellular Respiration

MS-LS1-6, MS-LS1-7

9. Which is a product of fermentation?
A. oxygen **B.** sugar
C. alcohol **D.** nitrogen

10. The second stage of cellular respiration takes place in the
A. mitochondria. **B.** root nodules.
C. chloroplast. **D.** atmosphere.

11. .... and .... can be considered opposite processes.
A. Fermentation, cellular respiration
B. Photosynthesis, nitrogen fixation
C. Evaporation, fermentation
D. Photosynthesis, cellular respiration

12. **Apply Scientific Reasoning** Why do you think plants hold on to a small amount of the oxygen produced during photosynthesis for use during cellular respiration?

$$\underset{\text{glucose}}{C_6H_{12}O_6} + \underset{\text{oxygen}}{6\,O_2} \longrightarrow \underset{\text{carbon dioxide}}{6\,CO_2} + \underset{\text{water}}{6\,H_2O} + \text{energy}$$

13. **Determine Similarities** How do the reactants of photosynthesis compare to the products of cellular respiration?

14. **SEP Evidence** Provide evidence to support the statement "Living systems cycle energy".

15. **SEP Construct Explanations** A certain type of fungus lives in environments where there is no oxygen. Would you expect this fungus to produce energy using cellular respiration or fermentation? Explain.

16. **SEP Develop Models** Create a flow chart that shows the stages of cellular respiration and the part of the cell each step occurs in. Be sure to include the following terms: Stage 1, Stage 2, glucose breakdown, oxygen, mitochondria, cytoplasm, energy, carbon dioxide, water.

17. **Explain Phenomenon** How do you think carbon is recycled between organisms and their environment?

TOPIC 1 Review and Assess

MS-LS1-6, MS-LS1-7

Evidence-Based Assessment

In late 2013, California was in the midst of a severe drought. Farms, ranches, and vineyards were suffering. Agriculture is an important part of the state's economy and it was suffering. In January 2014, the governor issued an official State of Emergency, with the goal of easing the impact of the drought on citizens, crops, and the environment. It stated that:

> *State agencies, led by the Department of Water Resources, will execute a statewide water conservation campaign to make all Californians aware of the drought and encourage personal actions to reduce water usage. This campaign will coordinate with local water agencies, [and] . . . call on Californians to reduce their water usage by 20 percent.*

Fortunately, the drought ended in late 2016. Governor Brown lifted the State of Emergency in April 2017. Estimating annual runoff helps to analyze the moisture level of an area to determine a drought. *Annual runoff* is water that is released by the land, or "runs off," in one year. Runoff is mostly precipitation that remains after water has evaporated, been used by plants, and seeped into soil. Runoff will make its way to bodies of water.

Annual California Runoff

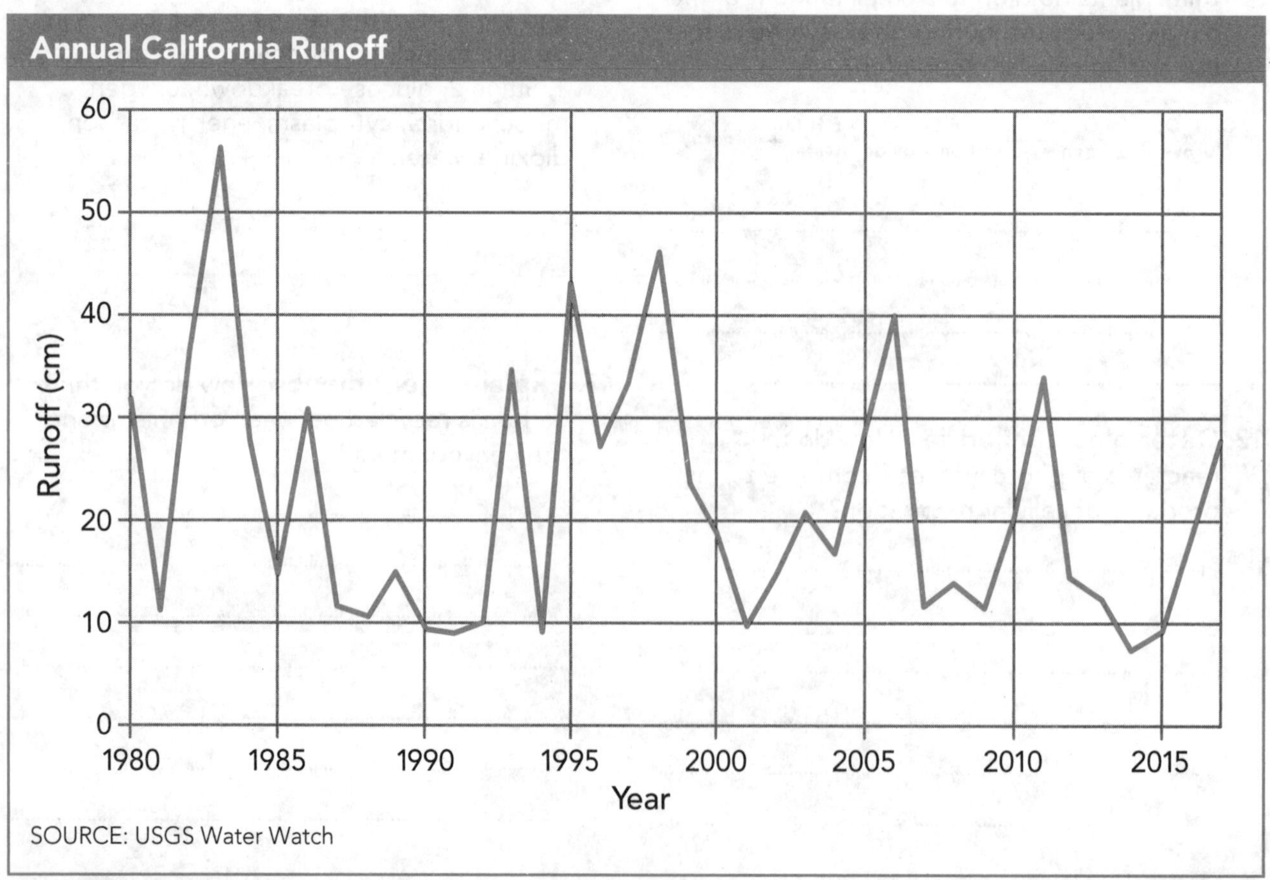

SOURCE: USGS Water Watch

Use the graph to answer the questions.

1. **SEP Interpret Data** What do the data indicate about California's climate?
   A. It is steadily becoming wetter.
   B. It is steadily becoming drier.
   C. It has wetter and drier cycles.
   D. It does not change.

2. **SEP Evaluate Evidence** Where does the water a land plant uses for photosynthesis come from? Why would that water be scarce during a drought? Select the answers to make the statement true.

   The water comes from ....
   A. evaporation B. condensation
   C. precipitation

   During a drought, soil is ....
   A. wetter B. drier

   due to ....
   A. excess rain or snow
   B. little rain or snow
   C. less water vapor in the air

3. **SEP Construct Explanations** If a plant is considered drought-resistant, does it require more water or less water to perform photosynthesis? Explain.

   ....

   ....

   ....

4. **Analyze Phenomenon** Low-lying areas like river valleys can dry out in droughts but may also flood in unusually rainy periods. Suppose you were a valley tomato farmer in California. Based on your knowledge of photosynthesis and the data, would you buy seeds that were regular, drought-resistant, flood-resistant, or some combination? Explain.

   ....

   ....

   ....

   ....

   ....

   ....

5. **CCC Energy and Matter** The processes of photosynthesis and cellular respiration are continually cycling matter: carbon dioxide, water, and oxygen. How can a drought affect both processes in that cycle? Select all that apply.
   - ☐ Less available water means photosynthesis slows down.
   - ☐ Less oxygen is produced, so more cellular respiration can occur.
   - ☐ Less oxygen is produced and cellular respiration slows down.
   - ☐ More cellular respiration occurs, producing more carbon dioxide.
   - ☐ Less carbon dioxide in the atmosphere can slow photosynthesis in plants.
   - ☐ Plants have more carbon dioxide and photosynthesis occurs at a faster rate.

Quest FINDINGS

Complete the Quest!

Phenomenon Create a plan of action to identify the steps your neighbor can take to solve the greenhouse problem.

CCC Systems Photosynthesis and cellular respiration play important roles in the cycling of matter and energy on Earth. How are plants and animals dependent on one another for survival?

....

....

....

....

....

INTERACTIVITY

Reflect on the Problem in the Greenhouse

uDemonstrate Lab

MS-LS1-6, MS-LS1-7

Cycling Energy and Matter

How can you **model** matter and energy moving **through** a **living system**?

Background

Phenomenon What's the farthest you've ever walked? How did you have the energy to walk that far? You probably know that you get energy from the food you eat. But where did the energy in your food come from? In this investigation, you will demonstrate how matter and energy move through a living system.

Materials

(per group)

- eight test tubes
- two test tube racks
- cardboard box
- four snails
- four Elodea
- for each test tube: approximately 30 mL of deionized water to cover the organisms and 3 mL of bromothymol blue
- grow light

Safety

Be sure to follow all safety guidelines provided by your teacher. The appendix of your textbook provides more details about the safety icons.

Demonstrate Go online for a downloadable worksheet of this lab.

Plan Your Investigation

1. Knowing that bromothymol blue turns yellow in the presence of carbon dioxide, discuss as a group how to design an investigation to answer these questions:
   - How can we determine whether cellular respiration or photosynthesis is taking place in an organism?
   - Using these two organisms, how can we model an ecosystem in which matter is recycled?
2. Predict any outcomes you expect and determine what you will be observing and what data you will be recording. Create a data table in the space provided.
3. Put the following items in each test tube as indicated:
   - **Suggestion:** Number the test tubes from 1–8. Arrange the odd-numbered test tubes in one group and the even-numbered test tubes in another group.

Test Tubes	Items
1 and 2	water only
3 and 4	two snails
5 and 6	two strands of Elodea
7 and 8	two snails and two strands of Elodea

Snails are animals that conduct cellular respiration.

4. In the space provided, briefly describe your investigation and the procedure you will follow.
5. Conduct your investigation. Remember to record your observations in your data table. Make observations after 24 hours as well.

Elodea is a plant that conducts photosynthesis in light. It also conducts cellular respiration.

Procedure

Data Table

Analyze and Interpret Data

1. **Identify Variables** The control group of this experiment consisted of the test tubes filled with only water. What is the purpose of this control group?

2. **SEP Analyze Data** Consider the two test tubes that contained strands of Elodea. What accounts for the difference in the colors of the liquid in the test tubes after 24 hours?

3. **Claim** What gas was present in the test tubes containing both Elodea and snails after 24 hours?

4. **Evidence** What evidence supports the presence of your claim in the test tubes containing both Elodea and snails?

5. **Reasoning** Explain how your evidence supports your claim for the test tubes containing both Elodea and snails.

6. **SEP Develop Models** Sketch a simple diagram of a snail and a strand of Elodea. Model how carbon dioxide and oxygen cycles between the plants and snails.

TOPIC 2

Ecosystems

LESSON 1
Living Things and the Environment
uInvestigate Lab: Elbow Room

LESSON 2
Energy Flow in Ecosystems
uInvestigate Lab: Observing Decomposition

uEngineer It! STEM **Eating Oil**

LESSON 3
Cycles of Matter
uInvestigate Lab: Following Water

NGSS PERFORMANCE EXPECTATIONS

MS-LS2-1 Analyze and interpret data to provide evidence for the effects of resource availability on organisms and populations of organisms in an ecosystem.

MS-LS2-3 Develop a model to describe the cycling of matter and flow of energy among living and nonliving parts of an ecosystem.

How are these manatees well suited to their environment?

uConnect Explore how you are part of a cycle on Earth.

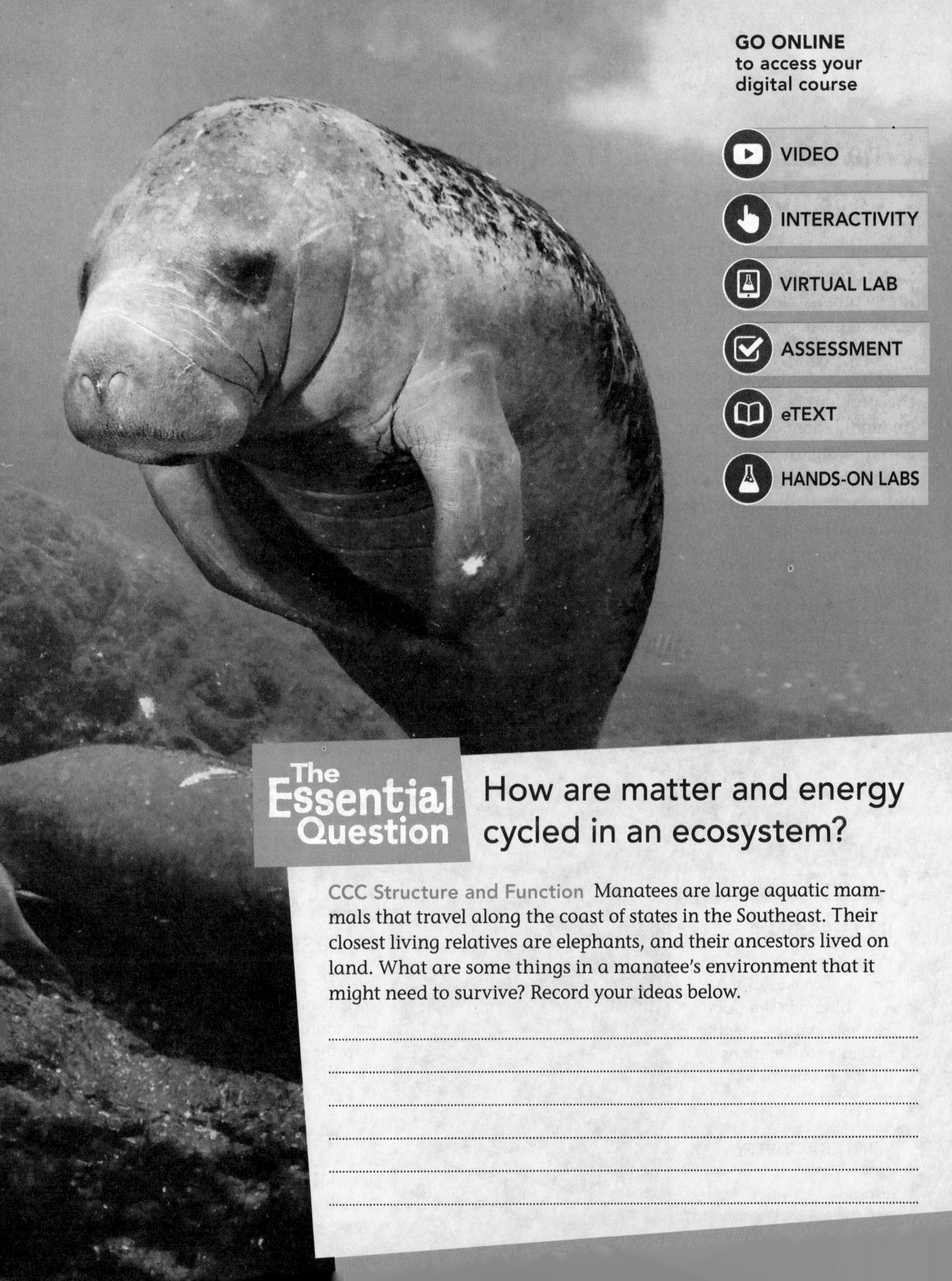

The Essential Question

How are matter and energy cycled in an ecosystem?

CCC Structure and Function Manatees are large aquatic mammals that travel along the coast of states in the Southeast. Their closest living relatives are elephants, and their ancestors lived on land. What are some things in a manatee's environment that it might need to survive? Record your ideas below.

....

....

....

....

....

....

Quest KICKOFF

What do you think is causing Pleasant Pond to turn green?

Phenomenon In 2016, algal blooms turned bodies of water green and slimy in Florida, Utah, California, and many other states. These blooms put people and ecosystems in danger. Scientists that study lakes and other inland bodies of water, known as limnologists, are working to predict and prevent future algal blooms. In this problem-based Quest activity, you will investigate an algal bloom at a lake and determine its cause. In labs and digital activities, you will apply what you learn in each lesson to help you gather evidence to solve the mystery. With enough evidence, you will be able to identify what you believe is the cause of the algal bloom and present a solution in the Findings activity.

INTERACTIVITY

Mystery at Pleasant Pond

MS-LS2-1 Analyze and interpret data to provide evidence for the effects of resource availability on organisms and populations of organisms in an ecosystem.
MS-LS2-3 Develop a model to describe the cycling of matter and flow of energy among living and nonliving parts of an ecosystem.

NBC LEARN VIDEO

After watching the above Quest Kickoff Video, which explores the effects of a toxic algal bloom in Lake Erie, think about the impact that shutting down the water supply might have on your community. Record your ideas below.

....

....

....

....

....

....

....

....

....

....

Quest CHECK-IN

IN LESSON 1

What are some possible causes of the algal bloom in the pond? Evaluate data to identify possible explanations for the problems at the pond.

INTERACTIVITY

Suspicious Activities

Quest CHECK-IN

IN LESSON 2

How do nutrients affect organisms in an aquatic environment? Investigate how the nonliving factors can affect the organisms in a pond.

INTERACTIVITY

Nutrients and Aquatic Organisms

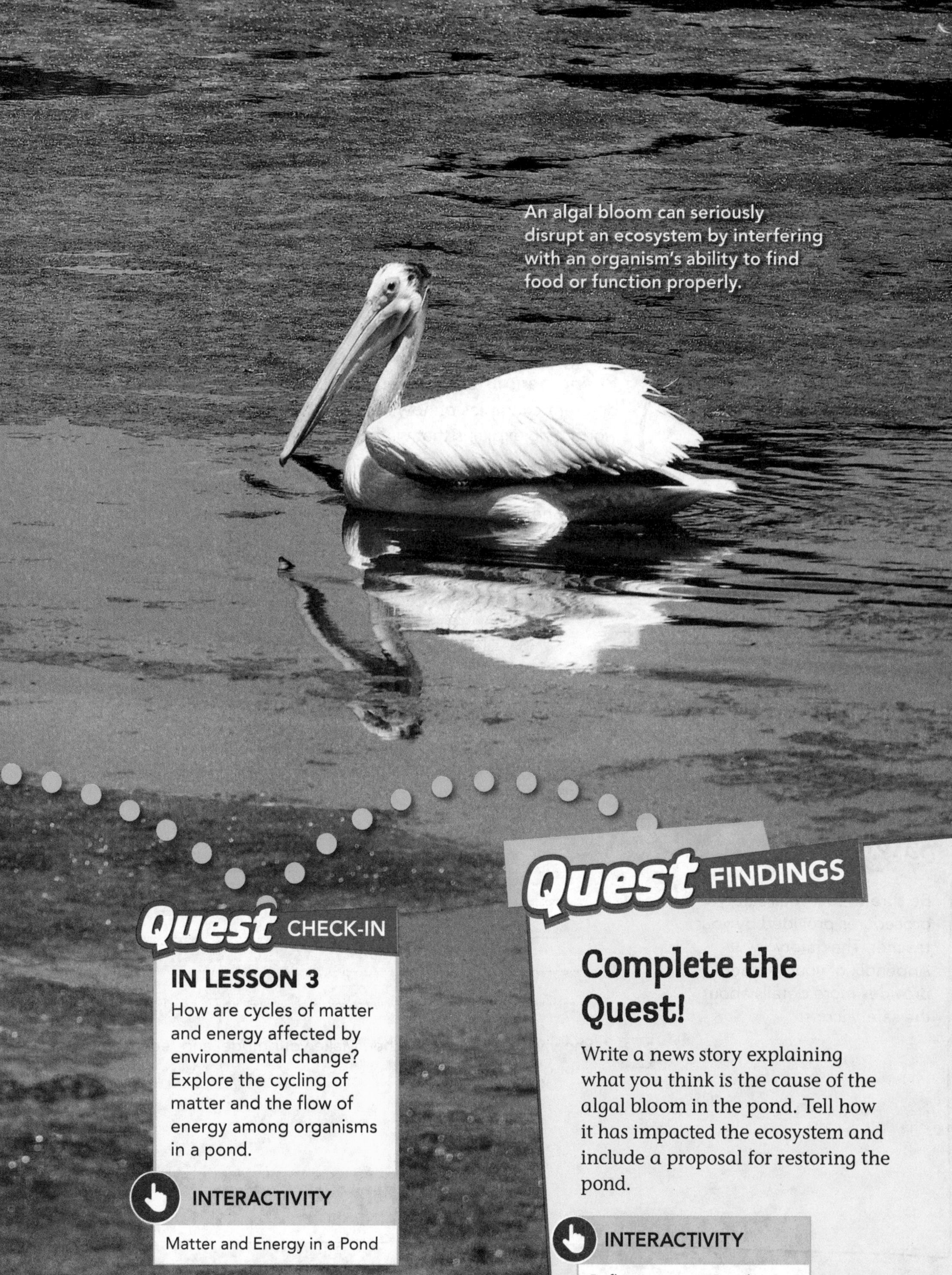

An algal bloom can seriously disrupt an ecosystem by interfering with an organism's ability to find food or function properly.

Quest CHECK-IN

IN LESSON 3

How are cycles of matter and energy affected by environmental change? Explore the cycling of matter and the flow of energy among organisms in a pond.

INTERACTIVITY

Matter and Energy in a Pond

Quest FINDINGS

Complete the Quest!

Write a news story explaining what you think is the cause of the algal bloom in the pond. Tell how it has impacted the ecosystem and include a proposal for restoring the pond.

INTERACTIVITY

Reflections on a Pond

uConnect Lab

MS-LS2-3

Every Breath You Take

How can you **develop a model** that shows the cycling of matter on Earth?

Background

Phenomenon Your teacher explains that there are many different examples of how matter is cycled throughout the world. She explains that water, rocks, and nutrients are a few examples of how matter moves in cycles. Your teacher tells you that even you are part of how matter is cycled on Earth. She challenges you to develop a model, using your breath as evidence that you are part of the cycling of matter on Earth.

Materials

(per group)

- small mirror

Safety

Be sure to follow all safety procedures provided by your teacher. The Safety Appendix of your textbook provides more details about the safety icons.

Design a Procedure

☐ 1. **SEP Develop a Model** Develop a model of how matter cycles on Earth. Write a plan that uses your breath and the mirror in the model.

....

....

....

....

....

....

☐ 2. Show your plan to a teacher. Make your model and record your observations.

Observations

uConnect Go online for a downloadable worksheet of this lab.

Analyze and Interpret Data

1. **Make a Claim** Write a claim about your role in the cycling of matter on Earth.

2. **SEP Use Evidence** Describe the evidence from your model that shows how matter flows in a cycle.

3. **SEP Construct Written Arguments** Based on your observations and evidence from your model, construct an explanation about how you are part of a cycle on Earth.

4. **SEP Develop Models** Draw a model that supports your explanation. Be sure to label each part of your model and use arrows to show how matter moves in the cycle.

LESSON

1 Living Things and the Environment

Guiding Questions

- How are populations affected by changes to the amount and availability of resources?
- How are population size and resource availability related?

Connections

Literacy Cite Textual Evidence

Math Represent Relationships

MS-LS2-1

HANDS-ON LAB

uInvestigate Model how space can be a limiting factor.

Vocabulary

organism
habitat
biotic factor
abiotic factor
population
community
ecosystem
limiting factor

Academic Vocabulary

resources
density

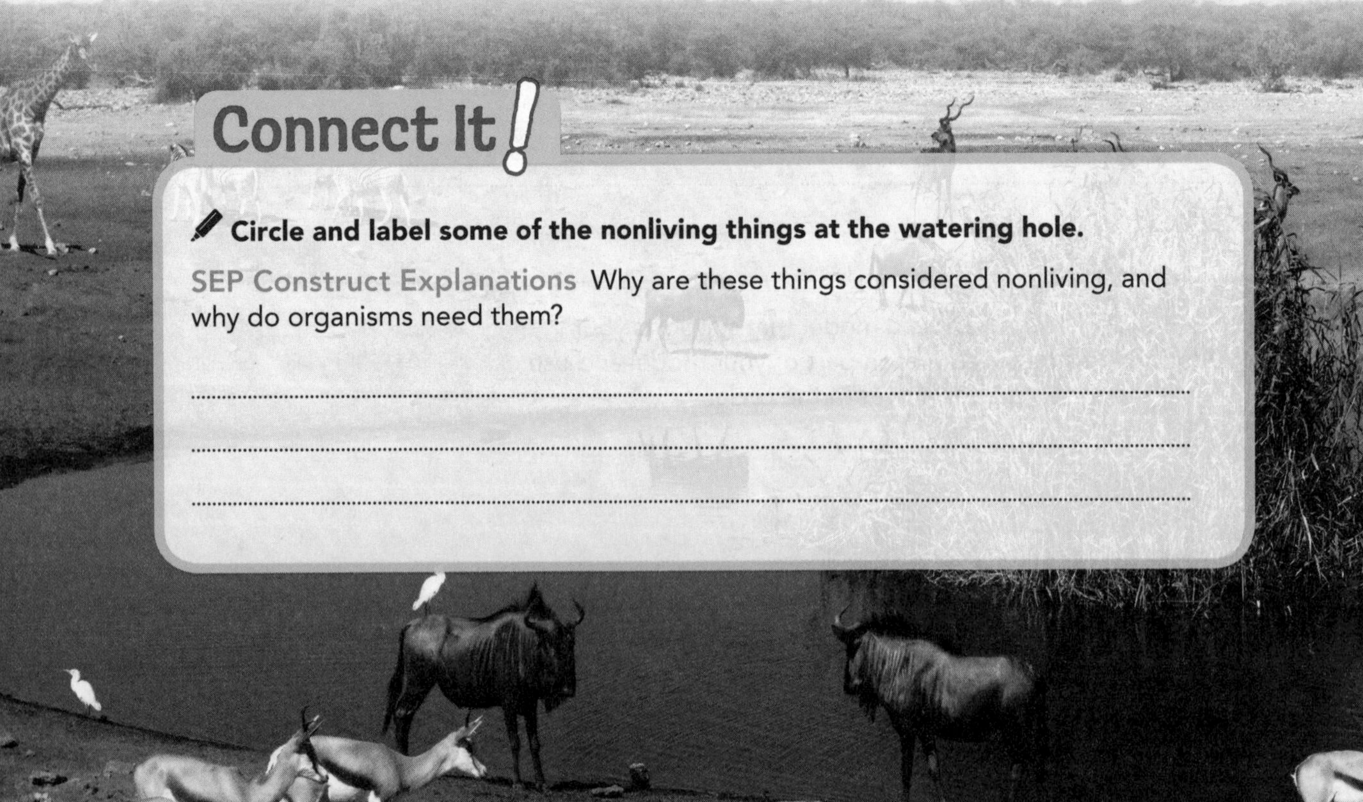

Connect It!

Circle and label some of the nonliving things at the watering hole.

SEP Construct Explanations Why are these things considered nonliving, and why do organisms need them?

Organisms and Habitats

Explore the relationships among living and nonliving things in a local area.

At the watering hole shown in **Figure 1**, animals such as giraffes stop to quench their thirst. A giraffe is an **organism**, or living thing. Different types of organisms live in different types of surroundings, or environments. An organism gets food, water, shelter, and other things from its environment that it needs to live, grow, and reproduce. These are called **resources**. An environment that provides the things a specific organism needs to live, grow, and reproduce is called a **habitat**.

In nature, every organism you see in a particular habitat is there because that habitat meets the organism's needs. Some organisms have the ability to move from one habitat to another as conditions change or as different needs arise, but many organisms stay in the same habitat for their entire lives. The living and nonliving things in a particular environment and the interactions among them define the habitat and its conditions.

Academic Vocabulary

Have you heard the term *resources* in other contexts? List some examples.

....

....

....

....

A Hangout in the Habitat

Figure 1 In any environment, like this watering hole in Etosha National Park in Namibia, Africa, living and nonliving things interact with each other.

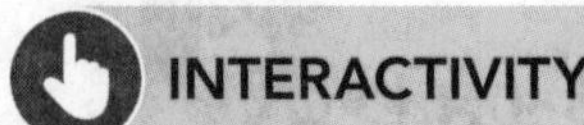

Explore the factors in a habitat.

Explore biotic and abiotic factors in everyday life.

Reflect What are some of the biotic and abiotic factors in the ecosystem in which you live?

Biotic Factors What types of living things are in the python's tropical rain forest habitat below (**Figure 2**)? The parts of a habitat that are or were once alive and that interact with an organism are called **biotic factors**. These biological components include the trees and plants. Animals that the python eats are biotic factors, as are the other snakes it encounters. Waste products made by these organisms and others are also considered biotic factors. Bacteria, mushrooms, and other small organisms are other types of biotic factors that play important roles in the habitat.

Abiotic Factors Organisms also interact with nonliving things in the environment. **Abiotic factors** are the nonliving parts of an organism's habitat. These physical components include water, oxygen, space, rocks, light, temperature, and soil. The quality and condition of the abiotic factors can have a major effect on living things. For example, water in a habitat may contain pollutants. The poor quality of the water may result in sickness or death for the organisms that live there.

READING CHECK **Cite Textual Evidence** Why do you think snakes do not live in the Arctic tundra? Use evidence from the text to support your answer.

....

....

Python Habitat

Figure 2 A python interacts with many biotic and abiotic factors in its habitat.

Design It!

There are different biotic and abiotic factors in a habitat.

SEP Develop Models Using common materials to model biotic and abiotic factors, draw a model of a local habitat. Include a key to identify what the different materials represent.

Levels of Organization
Figure 3 A single individual in an ecosystem is the organism, which forms a population with other members of its species. Different species form communities in a single ecosystem.

CCC Systems Make a prediction about how a lack of resources in an ecosystem might impact the levels of organization.

....

....

....

....

....

....

....

....

Ecosystem Organization

Most organisms do not live all alone in their habitat. Instead, organisms live together in populations and communities that interact with abiotic factors in their ecosystems. Interactions can also occur among the various populations. **Figure 3** summarizes the levels of organization in an ecosystem.

Organisms All of the Indian pythons that live in South Asia are members of one species. A species (SPEE sheez) is a group of organisms that can mate with each other and produce offspring that can also mate and reproduce.

Populations All the members of one species living in a particular area are referred to as a **population**. The Indian pythons of India's Keoladeo Ghana National Park, for example, are one example of a population.

Communities A particular area usually contains more than one species of organism. The Keoladeo Park is home to hundreds of bird species, as well as mammals, plants, and other varieties of organisms. All the different populations that live together in an area make up a **community**.

The community of organisms that lives in a particular area, along with the nonliving environment, make up an **ecosystem**. The study of how organisms interact with each other and with their environment is called ecology.

READING CHECK **Determine Meaning** What makes up a community in an ecosystem?

....

....

....

Literacy Connection

Cite Textual Evidence
Suppose farmers in an area spray insecticides on their crops. A population of birds that feeds on insects begins to decline. Underline the text that supports the idea that the insecticide may be responsible for the decline in the bird population.

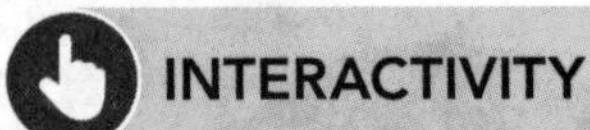

Analyze data to determine why a population has declined.

Populations

Remember from your reading that a population consists of all of the organisms of the same species living in the same area at the same time. For example, all of the pythons living in the same rainforest would be a distinct population. There are several things that can change a population's size.

Births and Deaths New individuals generally join a population by being born into it. A population grows when more individuals are born into it than die in any period of time. So when the birth rate (the number of births per 1,000 individuals for a given time period) is greater than the death rate (the number of deaths per 1,000 individuals for a given time period) a population may increase. When the birth rate is the same as the death rate, then the population usually remains stable. In situations where the death rate is greater than the birth rate, the population will decrease.

Graphing Population Changes

Changes over time in a population such as white-tailed deer in Ohio can be displayed in a graph.

Deer Population Trends, 2000–2010

Year	Population (estimated)	Year	Population (estimated)
2000	525,000	2006	770,000
2001	560,000	2007	725,000
2002	620,000	2008	745,000
2003	670,000	2009	750,000
2004	715,000	2010	710,000
2005	720,000		

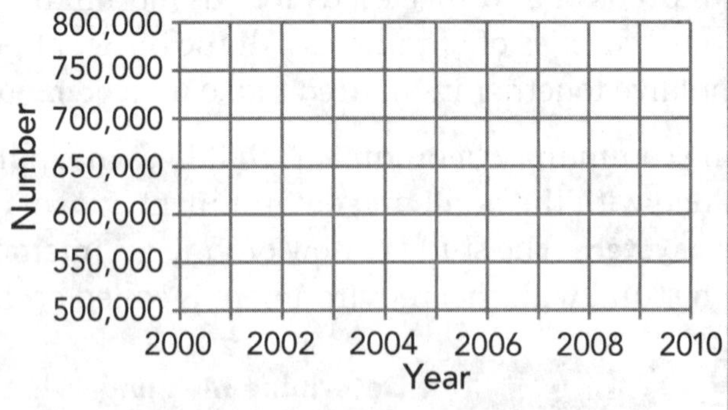

SOURCE: Ohio Department of Natural Resources

1. **Represent Relationships** Use the data table to complete a graph of the changes in the deer population. Then describe the trend in the graph.

2. **SEP Interpret Data** What factors do you think might be responsible for the changes in the deer population?

Immigration and Emigration

A population's size also can increase or decrease when individuals move into or out of the population. Immigration (im ih GRAY shun) means moving into a population. Emigration (em ih GRAY shun) means leaving a population. For instance, if food is scarce, some members of the antelope herd in **Figure 4** may wander off in search of a better habitat. If they become permanently separated from the original herd, they will no longer be part of that population.

Population Density

If you are a scientist studying an ecosystem or population, it can be helpful to know the population **density**—the number of individuals in an area of a specific size. Population density can be represented as an equation:

$$\text{Population density} = \frac{\text{Number of individuals}}{\text{Unit area}}$$

For example, suppose an ecologist estimates there are 800 beetles living in a park measuring 400 square meters. The population density would be 800 beetles per 400 square meters, or 2 beetles per square meter.

READING CHECK Summarize Text How do birth and death rates affect a population's size?

Investigate Model how space can be a limiting factor.

Academic Vocabulary

Have you heard the term *density* before? What did it mean in that other context?

Emigration

Figure 4 Food scarcity is just one cause of emigration. **SEP Construct Explanations** What other factors might cause individuals in this antelope herd to emigrate?

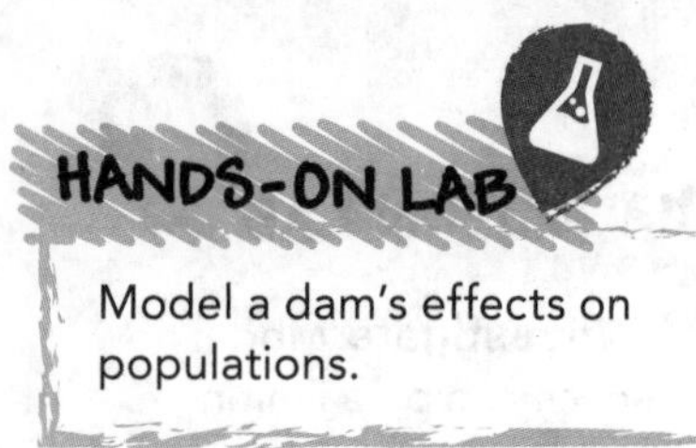

Model a dam's effects on populations.

Factors That Limit Population Growth

In general, a population grows if conditions are favorable. Eventually, however, some factor in the environment, such as the availability of food, will limit the size of a population. An environmental factor that causes a population to stop growing or to decrease in size, such as a fatal disease infecting organisms, organisms, is a **limiting factor**.

Food and Water Food and water can be limiting factors for virtually any population. An adult elephant eats an average of around 180 kilograms of vegetation each day to survive. Suppose the trees in its habitat can provide 1000 kilograms of vegetation daily. In this habitat, not more than 5 adult elephants could survive. The largest population that an area can support is called its carrying capacity.

Climate and Weather Changes in climate can limit population growth. Warmer weather in the early winter, for example, can cause some plants to continue growing. Natural disasters such as hurricanes and floods can have immediate and long-term effects on populations.

Space and Shelter Other limiting factors for populations are space and shelter, as illustrated by the nesting site in **Figure 5**. When individual organisms must compete for space to live or raise young, the population can decrease. Competition for suitable shelter also can limit the growth of a population.

READING CHECK **Summarize Text** How do limiting factors affect a population of organisms?

....

....

Limited Space

Figure 5 In the image of the gannets, circle or shade the available space in the environment for nesting and raising young.

CCC Cause and Effect How does the lack of space act as a limiting factor for these gannets?

....

....

....

....

....

....

LESSON 1 Check

MS-LS2-1

1. CCC Systems Identify the levels of organization in an ecosystem from smallest to largest.

Answer questions 2 and 3 using the graph below.

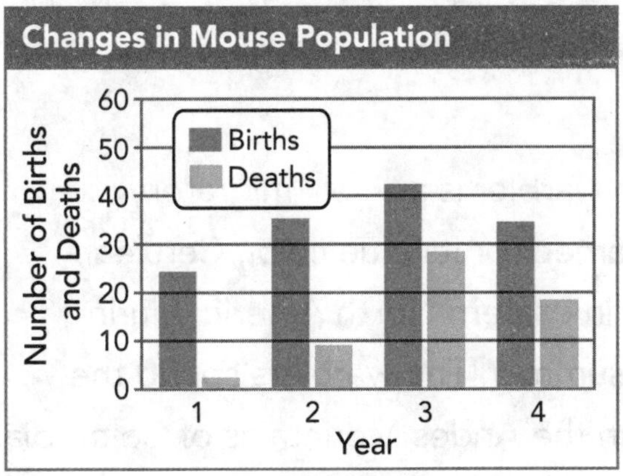

Changes in Mouse Population

Year	Births	Deaths
1	25	2
2	36	9
3	43	29
4	35	19

Number of Births and Deaths (0–60); Year

2. SEP Analyze Data What trends do you observe in the mouse population for the four years?

3. SEP Interpret Data Does the data support the idea that this population is relatively stable? Give evidence to support your answer.

4. SEP Construct Explanations How can biotic and abiotic factors in an ecosystem affect populations? Give two examples of each.

5. CCC Stability and Change Why is climate considered to be a limiting factor for populations in an ecosystem?

Quest CHECK-IN

In this lesson, you learned how ecosystems are organized and how different factors affect populations.

CCC Cause and Effect What effect might an algal bloom in a pond have on populations of organisms that make their home there?

INTERACTIVITY

Suspicious Activities

Go online to research and explore explanations for the algal bloom. Then, using the information you have gathered, identify three possible causes for the bloom.

Case Study

MS-LS2-1

THE CASE OF THE DISAPPEARING Cerulean Warbler

The cerulean warbler is a small, migratory songbird named for its blue color. Cerulean warblers breed in eastern North America during the spring and summer. The warblers spend the winter months in the Andes Mountains of Colombia, Venezuela, Ecuador, and Peru in northern part of South America.

The population of cerulean warblers is decreasing very quickly. No other population of songbirds is decreasing more rapidly in eastern North America. Populations of warblers have been declining at a rate of about 3 percent a year. This means that there are 3 percent fewer warblers from one year to the next. Habitat loss, especially in the region where the birds spend the winter, is thought to be the main reason. Look at the Cerulean Warbler Range Map.

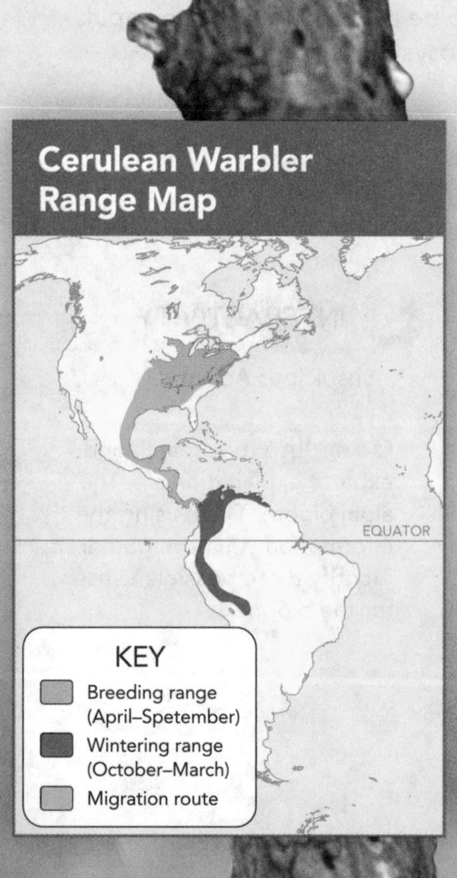

Habitat Loss in the Wintering Range

By 2025, there will be 100 million more people in South America than there were in 2002. As human population size increases, the demands on the land and local habitats also increase. Forests are cleared and habitats for native plants and animals are lost to make room for planting crops and for raising cattle. These crops and cattle are needed to feed the increased population of people in the area.

Cerulean warblers inhabit the dense, evergreen forests that grow at middle elevations in the Andes Mountains. Their preferred habitat is tall, mature trees where they can feed on insects.

However, this habitat is also the preferred area to grow shade-coffee crops. The tall trees provide shade for the shorter coffee plants. Shade-coffee takes longer to grow and produces less coffee than sun-grown coffee crops. Forested areas are often cleared to make room for sun-grown coffee and other more profitable crops needing direct sunlight. This reduces the size of the warbler's habitat. As shown in the graph, the rate of clearing has decreased in recent years because the forests that are left are on steep slopes. These steep slopes and high elevations are not suitable for farming. Look at the bar graph below.

Use the graph to answer the following questions.

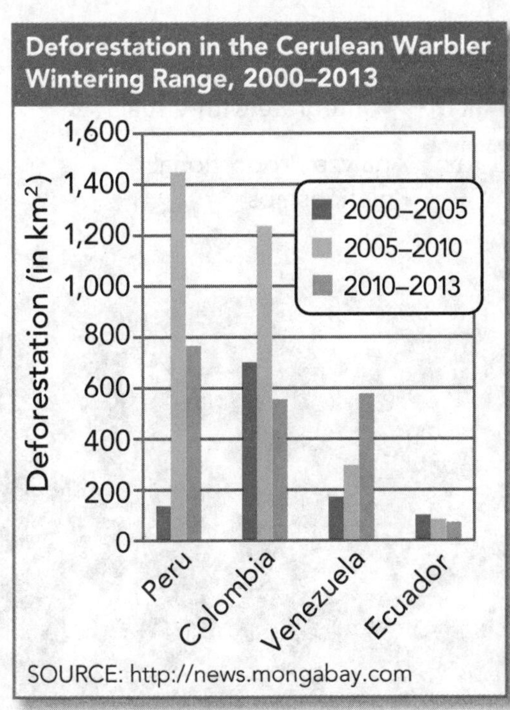

1. CCC Patterns Describe any patterns you see in the graph.

2. Predict What do you think the data will look like for each country until 2020? Why?

3. SEP Construct Explanations Explain how you think changing levels of deforestation in the wintering range affects the cerulean warbler population.

4. SEP Design Solutions What are some strategies that you think can be used in northern South America to stabilize and protect the warbler populations?

LESSON

2 Energy Flow in Ecosystems

Guiding Questions

- What are the energy roles in an ecosystem?
- How is energy transferred between living and nonliving parts of an ecosystem?
- How is energy conserved in an ecosystem?

Connections

Literacy Integrate with Visuals

Math Analyze Proportional Relationships

MS-LS2-3

HANDS-ON LAB

uInvestigate Observe how decomposers get energy.

Vocabulary

producer
consumer
decomposer
food chain
food web
energy pyramid

Academic Vocabulary

role

Connect It!

Shade in one of the arrows to indicate the direction in which energy flows between the frog and the fly.

CCC Energy and Matter Where do you think the plants in the image get the energy they need to grow and survive?

....

....

....

Energy Roles in an Ecosystem

Identify the sources of your dinner.

In gym class, have you ever been assigned to play a position like catcher or goalie for your class team? If so, you know what it's like to have a specific **role** in a system. Similar to positions in sports, every organism has a role in the movement of energy through its ecosystem.

Energy roles are based on the way organisms obtain food and interact with other organisms. In an ecosystem, organisms play the energy role of either a producer, consumer, or decomposer.

Academic Vocabulary

Have you heard the term *role* in other contexts? List some examples.

....

....

....

Producers

Energy enters most ecosystems as sunlight. Some organisms, such as the plants shown in **Figure 1** and some types of bacteria, capture the energy of sunlight. These organisms use the sun's energy to recombine atoms from molecules of water and carbon dioxide into food molecules in a process called photosynthesis.

An organism that can make its own food is a **producer**. Producers become the source of food for other organisms in an ecosystem. In a few ecosystems, producers obtain energy from a source other than sunlight. Deep in the ocean, some bacteria convert chemical energy into food from hydrothermal vents in the ocean floor. They are the producers in these ecosystems that include worms, clams, and crabs.

Obtaining Energy

Figure 1 Many small pond organisms, like the fly, obtain energy from green plants. They, in turn, serve to provide energy for larger organisms, like the frog.

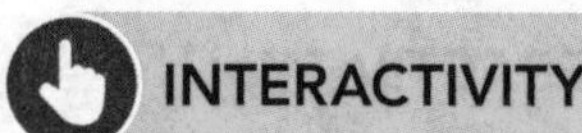

INTERACTIVITY

Model energy roles and energy flow in ecosystems.

INTERACTIVITY

Explore the roles living things play in ecosystems.

Write About It What are some producers, consumers, scavengers, and decomposers you have seen in your neighborhood?

Consumers Organisms like the animals in **Figure 2** cannot produce their own food. A **consumer** obtains energy by feeding on other organisms.

Scientists classify consumers according to what they eat. As consumers eat, the food is broken down into molecules that help supply them energy.

Consumers that eat only animals are carnivores. Great white sharks, owls, and tigers are examples of carnivores. Some carnivores are scavengers. A scavenger is a carnivore that feeds on the bodies of dead organisms. Scavengers include hagfish and condors. Some carnivores will scavenge if they cannot find live animals to prey upon.

Herbivores are consumers that eat only plants and other photosynthetic organisms. Grasshoppers, rabbits, and cows are herbivores.

Consumers that eat both plants and animals are omnivores. Raccoons, pigs, and humans are omnivores.

Life and Death in an Alaskan Stream

Figure 2 Salmon migrate upstream to this forest environment after spending most of their lives at sea. As they travel, many of them become food for the ecosystem's carnivores.

SEP Develop Models Label the producers, consumers, decomposers, and scavengers in the image.

Investigate Observe how decomposers get energy.

Decomposers If the only roles in an ecosystem were producer and consumer, then some of the matter that is essential for life, such as carbon and nitrogen, would remain in the waste products and remains of dead organisms. However, decomposers have a role in ecosystems to prevent this from happening. **Decomposers** break down biotic wastes and dead organisms, returning the raw materials to the ecosystem. For example, after adult salmon swim upstream and reproduce, they die. Their carcasses litter the riverbeds and banks. Bacteria in the soil help break down the carcasses, releasing their nutrients to trees, grasses, shrubs, and other producers that depend on them.

In a sense, decomposers are nature's recyclers. While obtaining energy for their own needs, decomposers also return matter in the form of simple molecules to the environment. These molecules can be used again by other organisms. Mushrooms, bacteria, and mold are common decomposers.

READING CHECK **Integrate with Visuals** In terms of their energy roles, what similarities do the bear, salmon, and coyote in **Figure 2** share?

....

....

Food chain

Grizzly bear

Salmon

Crustaceans

Zooplankton

Phytoplankton

Energy and Matter Transfer

Energy in most ecosystems comes from sunlight, and producers convert this energy into food through photosynthesis. The energy and matter are contained in atoms and molecules that are transferred to herbivores that eat the producers. Then they move on to carnivores feeding on the first, or primary, consumers. The energy and matter next move on through other meat-eating secondary consumers. This movement of energy and matter can be described through different models: food chains, food webs, and energy pyramids.

Food Chains A food chain is one way to show how energy and matter move through an ecosystem. A **food chain** is a series of events in which one organism eats another and obtains energy and nutrients. **Figure 3** illustrates one example of a food chain. The arrows indicate the movement of energy and matter as organisms are consumed up the food chain.

Food Webs Energy and matter move in one direction through a food chain, but they can also take different paths through the ecosystem. However, most producers and consumers are part of many overlapping food chains. For example, a salmon could be consumed by a shark in the ocean before it even has the chance to migrate upstream and encounter a bear. A more realistic way to show how energy and matter cycle through an ecosystem is with a food web. As shown in **Figure 4**, a **food web** consists of many overlapping food chains in an ecosystem.

Organisms may play more than one role in an ecosystem. Look at the crayfish in **Figure 4**. A crayfish is an omnivore that is a first-level consumer when it eats plants. However, when a crayfish eats a snail, it is a second-level consumer.

Food Chain

Figure 3 The food chain tracing a path from the phytoplankton to the grizzly bear is a simple way of showing how energy and matter flow from one organism to the next in the Alaskan stream ecosystem shown in **Figure 2**.

CCC System Models What are some limitations of modeling the flow of energy and matter in an ecosystem with a food chain?

Model It!

Food Web

Figure 4 This food web depicts relationships among some of the organisms that live in a forest that has a small pond.

SEP Develop Models Complete the food web by drawing and identifying the missing organisms listed below. Add arrows to the diagram to complete the web.

mushrooms **red fox** **snail** **garter snake**

Third-level consumers eat the second-level consumers.

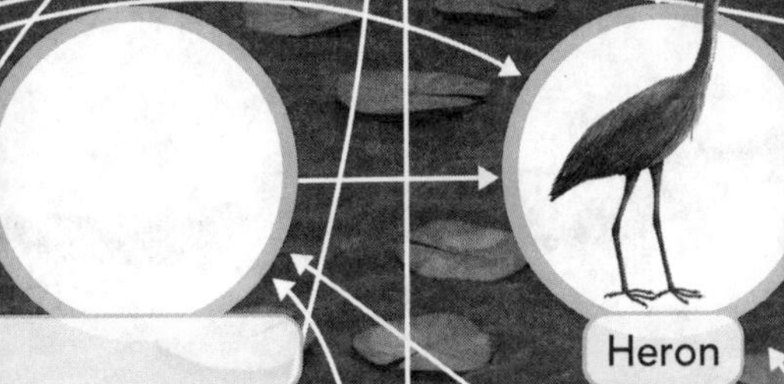

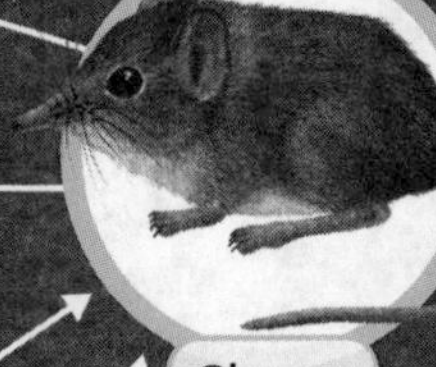

Second-level consumers eat the first-level consumers.

First-level consumers are organisms that feed directly on the producers.

Producers form the base of the food web.

Decomposers break down the wastes and remains of other organisms.

Investigate the food web of Chesapeake Bay.

Literacy Connection

Integrate with Visuals
Why is an energy pyramid shaped like a triangle with the point on top?

....

....

....

....

Energy Pyramids A diagram called an **energy pyramid** shows the amount of energy that moves from one feeding level to another in a food web. Each step in a food chain or food web is represented by a level within an energy pyramid, as shown in **Figure 5**. Producers have the most available energy so they make up the first level, or base, of the pyramid. Energy moves up the pyramid from the producers, to the first-level consumers, to the second-level consumers and so on. There is no limit to the number of levels in a food web or an energy pyramid. However, the more levels that exist between a producer and a given consumer, the smaller the percentage of the original energy from the producers that is available to that consumer. Each level has less energy available than the level below.

When an organism consumes food it obtains energy and matter used to carry out life activities. These activities produce heat, which is released and lost to the environment, reducing the amount of energy available to the next level.

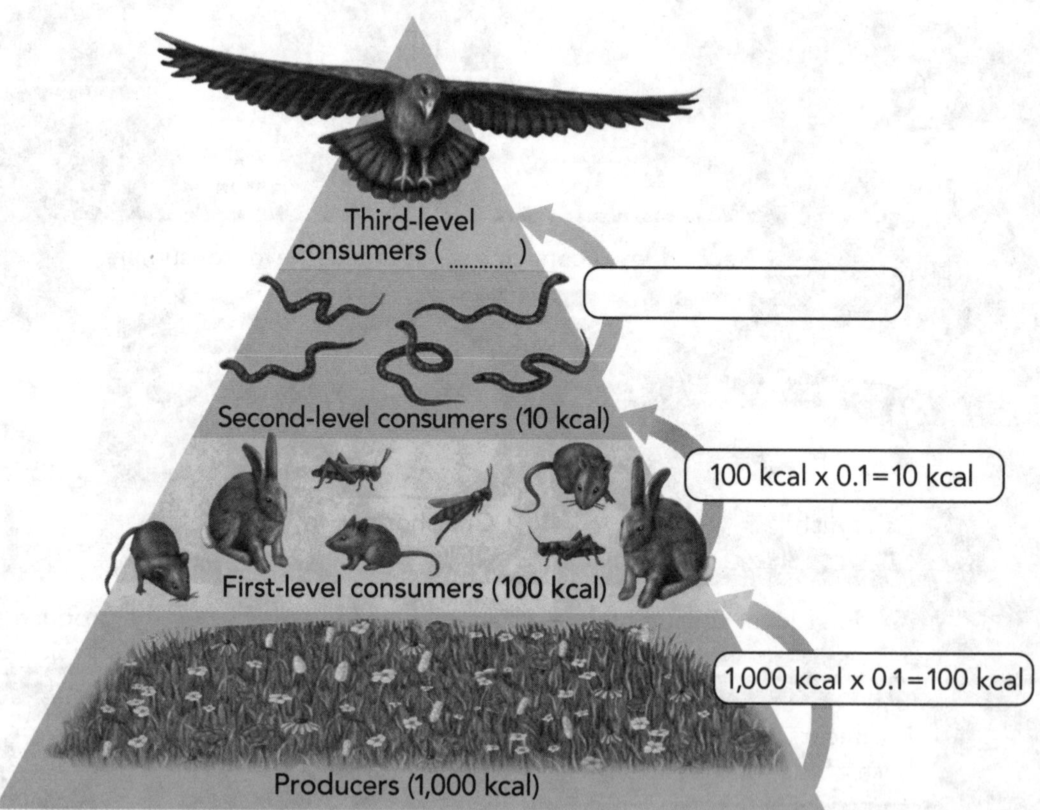

Energy Pyramid

Figure 5 This energy pyramid shows how the amount of available energy decreases as you move up an energy pyramid from the producers to the different levels of consumers. Only about 10 percent of the energy is transferred from level to level. Energy is measured in kilocalories, or kcal.

SEP Use Mathematics Write in the missing equation and fill in the energy that gets to the hawk at the top.

Energy Availability As you can see in **Figure 5**, only about 10 percent of the energy at one level of a food web is available to the next higher level. This greatly limits how many different levels a food chain can have, as well as the numbers of organisms that can be supported at higher levels. This is why it is typical for there to be fewer organisms as you move from one level of a pyramid or one "link" in a food chain up to the next level.

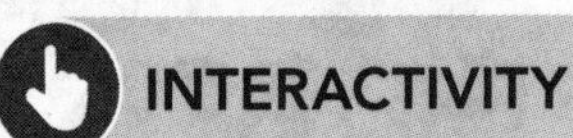

Model how altering a food web affects the flow of energy and matter in an ecosystem.

READING CHECK **Summarize Text** Why is energy reduced at each level of the energy pyramid?

....

....

....

Math Toolbox

Relationships in an Energy Pyramid

In a small forest ecosystem, caterpillars eat plants. Carolina wrens eat the caterpillars, and black rat snakes eat the wrens. Suppose that the plants contain 550,000 kilocalories.

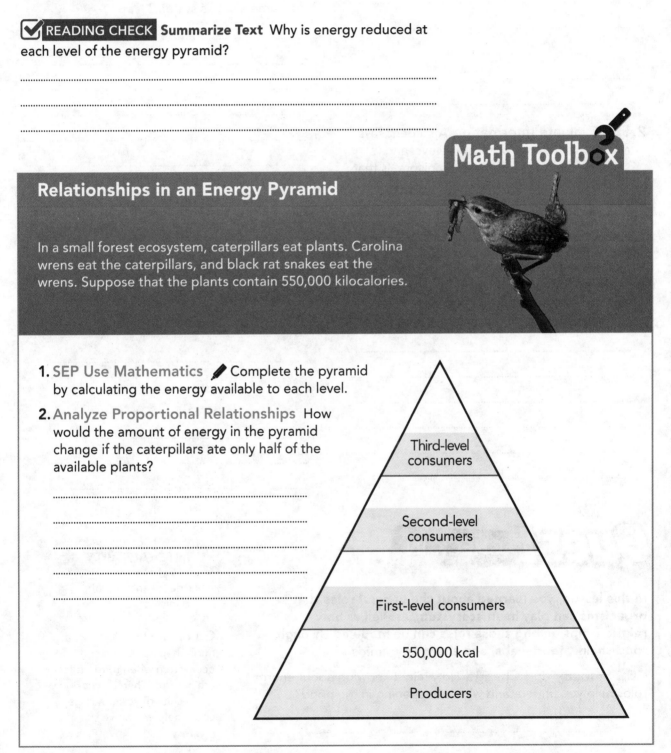

1. **SEP Use Mathematics** Complete the pyramid by calculating the energy available to each level.
2. **Analyze Proportional Relationships** How would the amount of energy in the pyramid change if the caterpillars ate only half of the available plants?

....

....

....

....

....

Third-level consumers

Second-level consumers

First-level consumers

550,000 kcal

Producers

LESSON 2 Check

MS-LS2-3

1. **CCC System Models** Which model best illustrates the flow of energy and matter in an ecosystem—a food chain or a food web? Explain.

2. **SEP Evaluate Information** A student says an organism that is both a first-level and second-level consumer is an omnivore. Is that student correct? Explain.

3. **CCC Energy and Matter** Suppose a rancher wants to buy some grassland to raise cattle. What should she know about energy flow before she invests in the land or the cattle?

4. **CCC Patterns** In Massachusetts, a team of scientists studying great white sharks estimates that a population of 15,000 seals supports fewer than 100 sharks during the summer. Why are there so few top-level consumers in this system?

5. **SEP Construct Explanations** Human activity can affect ecosystems by removing producers, consumers, and decomposers. What limiting factors may result from human actions, and what effects might they have on the flow of energy and matter in an ecosystem?

Quest CHECK-IN

In this lesson, you learned about the general roles that organisms can play in an ecosystem, as well as how relationships among those roles can be modeled through food chains, food webs, and energy pyramids.

CCC Stability and Change How might knowing about energy roles help you understand what's happening in the pond?

INTERACTIVITY

Nutrients and Aquatic Organisms

Go online to analyze what might happen to a pond ecosystem when nutrient levels are altered. Then discuss how the results of your analysis could help you solve the mystery.

uEngineer It! Sustainable Design STEM

MS-LS2-1, MS-LS2-3

Eating Oil

Do you know how tiny organisms can clean up oil spills? You engineer it! Strategies used to deal with the Deepwater Horizon oil spill, the worst in U.S. history, show us how.

The Challenge: To clean up harmful oil from marine environments

Phenomenon On April 20, 2010, part of an oil rig in the Gulf of Mexico exploded. It leaked oil for 87 days. By the time the leak was fixed, about 200 million gallons of oil had spilled into the water. Oil destroys beaches, marshlands, and marine ecosystems. It coats birds, fish, and marine animals, such as dolphins and sea turtles. The oil makes it difficult for many animals to move and get food, and causes others to suffocate.

Ecologists engineered a solution that relied on nature to help with the cleanup. They poured chemicals into the water that helped break up the oil into smaller droplets. Then the bacteria and fungi in the water broke down the oil droplets.

Bioremediation uses natural living things to reduce contaminants in an environment. In the event of an oil spill, oil-eating populations of bacteria and fungi grow quickly. Now, scientists are working to engineer ways to increase the speed at which these decomposers work and to make sure the oceans can support optimal populations of these tiny oil eaters.

INTERACTIVITY

Design your own method to clean up an oil spill.

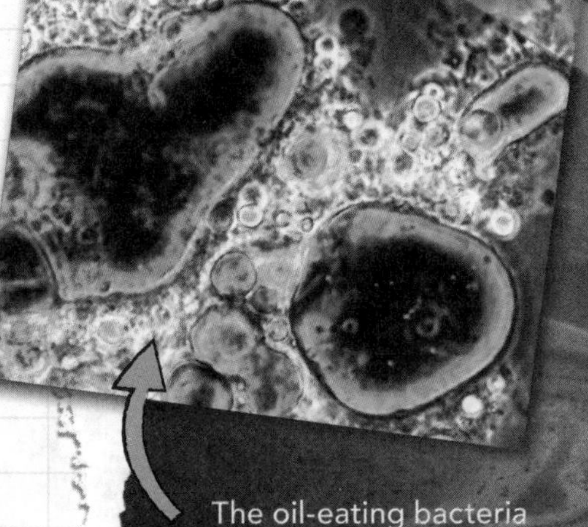

The oil-eating bacteria helped in the cleanup after the Deepwater Horizon oil spill.

DESIGN CHALLENGE

Can you put decomposers to work and build your own composter? Go to the Engineering Design Notebook to find out!

LESSON

3 Cycles of Matter

Guiding Questions

- How is matter transferred between the living and nonliving parts of an ecosystem?
- How is matter conserved in an ecosystem?

Connections

Literacy Determine Central Ideas

Math Analyze Relationships

MS-LS2-3

HANDS-ON LAB

uInvestigate Model the water cycle.

Vocabulary

Law of Conservation of Mass
Law of Conservation of Energy
evaporation
condensation
precipitation

Academic Vocabulary

system
components

Connect It!

Draw arrows on Figure 1 and label them to show how energy enters or leaves the terrarium.

CCC Cause and Effect What would happen to the ecosystem in the terrarium if it were a closed system for energy?

....

....

SEP Explain Phenomena Why is this ecosystem considered a closed system and how could that system be changed?

....

....

....

Conservation of Matter and Energy

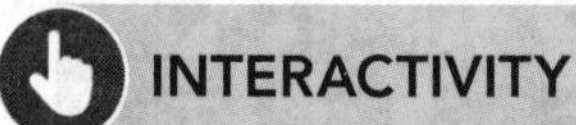

Consider your role in the cycling of energy.

During photosynthesis and cellular respiration, matter (mass) and energy can only change form. **The Law of Conservation of Mass** states that matter is neither created nor destroyed during any chemical or physical change. **The Law of Conservation of Energy** states that when one form of energy is transformed to another, no energy is lost in the process. Energy cannot be created or destroyed, but it can change from one form to another.

The terrarium in **Figure 1** is a closed **system** for matter. Matter cannot enter or exit. The plants, soil, rocks, water, microorganisms, animals, and air in the terrarium are all **components** of the system. The components may change over time, but their total mass will remain the same. All over Earth, mass and energy are cycling through different forms without being created or destroyed.

Academic Vocabulary

The schools in one area are often called a *school system*. What are some of the *components* of this system?

....

....

....

....

READING CHECK **Distinguish Facts** What would you tell a classmate who claims that food is destroyed when you eat it?

....

....

Ecosystem in a Jar

Figure 1 After it is sealed, a terrarium becomes a closed system for matter. But energy can still flow in and out through the glass.

Spring Water

Figure 2 The water at Yellow Springs is high in iron, which stains the rocks orange.

Water Cycle

Recall that matter is made up of tiny particles called atoms and two or more atoms can join to make a molecule. Two hydrogen atoms combined with one oxygen atom forms a molecule of water.

Water is essential for life. Water cycles in a continuous process from Earth's surface to the atmosphere and back, in various forms, or states. The water cycle involves the processes of evaporation, condensation, and precipitation. Follow along on **Figure 3** as you read about each process to explore it in more detail.

Evaporation Water molecules move from Earth's surface up to the atmosphere by evaporation. **Evaporation** is the process by which molecules at the surface of liquid water absorb enough energy to change to a gas. This water vapor rises into the atmosphere. The energy needed for evaporation comes from sunlight. Water evaporates from oceans, lakes, fields, and other places. Smaller amounts of water also evaporate from living things. For example, plants release water vapor from their leaves. In addition, animals release liquid water in their wastes and water vapor when they exhale. You may recall that one of the products of cellular respiration is water.

Model It!

Where does your water come from?

Yellow Springs, Ohio, shown in **Figure 2**, has been a source of refreshing water for animals and people for centuries. Geologists studying the Yellow Spring have determined that the spring is fed by rain that falls only a few miles north. After the rain soaks into the ground, it travels underground for 12 to 18 months before flowing out of the spring.

SEP Develop Models Does your drinking water come from a central water supply, a well, or bottles? Identify the source of your water and trace its origin back as far as you can. Make a model of the path the water takes to get to your home.

Condensation Rising water vapor reaches a point in the atmosphere where it cools. As it cools, it turns back into small droplets of water in a liquid state. The process of a gas changing to a liquid is **condensation.** The water droplets collect around dust particles and eventually form clouds. Dew is water that has condensed on plants or other objects on a cool morning.

Investigate Model the water cycle.

Precipitation Condensing water vapor collects as clouds, but as the drops continue to grow larger, they become heavier. Eventually the heavy drops fall in the form of **precipitation:** rain, snow, sleet, or hail. Precipitation can fall into oceans, lakes, or rivers. Precipitation falling on land may soak into the soil and become groundwater, or it may run off the land and flow into rivers or oceans.

Write About It Think how you interacted with water today. Where did that water come from? Where did it go next? Write a story that traces the water molecule's trip.

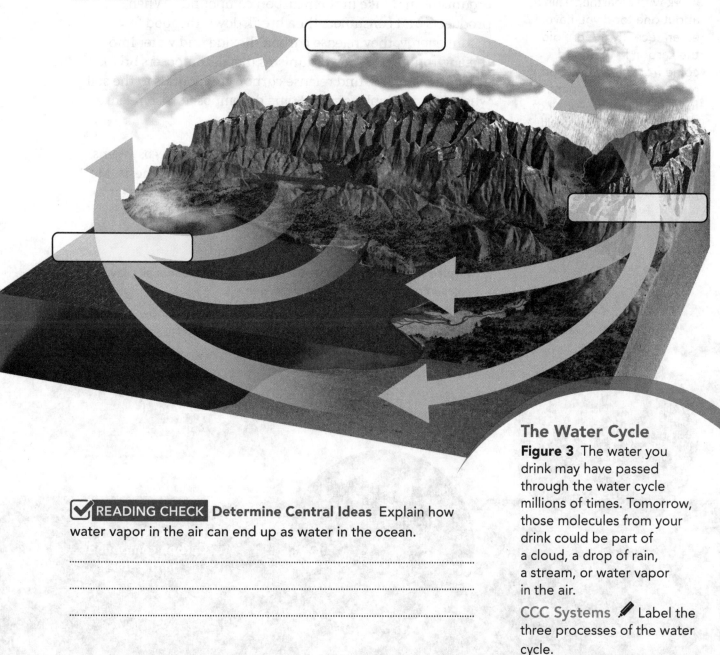

The Water Cycle

Figure 3 The water you drink may have passed through the water cycle millions of times. Tomorrow, those molecules from your drink could be part of a cloud, a drop of rain, a stream, or water vapor in the air.

CCC Systems Label the three processes of the water cycle.

READING CHECK **Determine Central Ideas** Explain how water vapor in the air can end up as water in the ocean.

....

....

....

Carbon and Oxygen Cycles

Carbon and oxygen are essential for life. Carbon is the building block of living things. For example, carbon is a major component of bones and the proteins that build muscles. Most organisms also use oxygen for their life processes. **Figure 4** shows how carbon and oxygen cycles in ecosystems are linked. Producers, consumers, and decomposers all play roles in recycling carbon and oxygen.

Carbon Cycle Most producers take in carbon dioxide gas from the air during photosynthesis. Producers use the carbon to make food—carbon-containing molecules, such as sugars and starches. Carbon is also converted by plants to compounds that help plants grow. Consumers eat other organisms and take in their carbon compounds. When producers and consumers then break down the food to obtain energy, they release carbon dioxide and water into the environment. When organisms die, decomposers break down the remains, and release carbon compounds to the soil where it is available for use. Some decomposers also release carbon dioxide into the air.

Oxygen Cycle Oxygen also cycles through ecosystems. Producers release oxygen as a product of photosynthesis. Most organisms take in oxygen from the air or water and use it to carry out cellular respiration.

Literacy Connection

Determine Central Ideas Work with a partner. Think about one food you have eaten recently. Where did the carbon in that food come from? Was the food made from plants, animals, fungi, or bacteria—or all of those sources? Where will the carbon go now that you have eaten the food? Share your response with another pair of students.

The Carbon and Oxygen Cycles

Figure 4 Producers, consumers, and decomposers all play roles in recycling carbon and oxygen.

SEP Develop Models Draw arrows to show how carbon and oxygen move through the ecosystem.

Law of Conservation On Earth, the number of carbon and oxygen atoms remains constant. Recall that atoms are not created or destroyed in chemical reactions. According to the Law of Conservation of Mass, atoms may appear in different chemical compounds as they get recycled through Earth's various systems, but they are never created or destroyed.

Human Impact Some human activities affect the levels of carbon and oxygen in the air. When humans burn gasoline, natural gas, and plant fuels, carbon dioxide is released into the atmosphere. Carbon dioxide levels also rise when humans clear forests to create farmland or to use the wood for lumber or fuel.

When trees are removed from an ecosystem, there are fewer producers to absorb carbon dioxide. If fallen trees are left on the ground, decomposers will break down their tissues through cellular respiration and release carbon dioxide into the air. Burning the trees has the same effect, because carbon dioxide is produced during combustion.

READING CHECK **Summarize Text** Describe the roles of producers and consumers in the oxygen cycle.

....

....

....

INTERACTIVITY

Investigate and identify the cycles of matter.

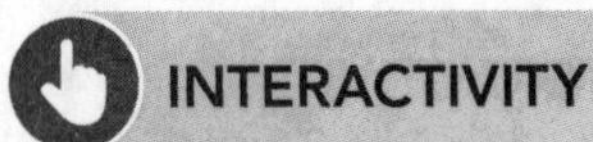

INTERACTIVITY

Explore and identify Earth's recyclables.

Nitrogen Cycle in Ecosystems

Like carbon, nitrogen is one of the necessary elements of life. Nitrogen is an important component for building proteins in animals and an essential nutrient for plants. In the nitrogen cycle, nitrogen moves from the air into the soil, into living things, and back into the air or soil. The air around you is about 78 percent nitrogen gas (N_2). However, most organisms cannot use nitrogen gas. Nitrogen gas is called "free" nitrogen because it is not combined with other kinds of atoms.

Nitrogen Fixation Most organisms can use nitrogen only after it has been "fixed," or combined with other elements to form nitrogen-containing compounds. Nitrogen fixation is the process of changing free nitrogen into a usable form of nitrogen, as shown in **Figure 5**. Certain bacteria perform most nitrogen fixation. These bacteria live in bumps called nodules on the roots of legume plants. Clover, beans, peas, alfalfa, peanuts, and trees such as mesquite and desert ironwood are all common legume plants. Nitrogen can also be "fixed" by lightning. About 10 percent of the nitrogen needed by plants is fixed by lightning.

Nitrogen Cycle

Figure 5 In the nitrogen cycle, free nitrogen from the air is fixed into compounds. Consumers can then use these nitrogen compounds to carry out their life processes.

CCC System Models
Circle the steps where free nitrogen is changed to a form plants and animals can use.

Free nitrogen in the air
Consumers eat nitrogen compounds in plants.
Plants use simple nitrogen compounds to make proteins and other complex compounds.
Decomposers return simple nitrogen compounds to the soil.
Bacteria in root nodules fix free nitrogen into simple compounds.
Soil bacteria release some free nitrogen into the air.
Fixed nitrogen in soil

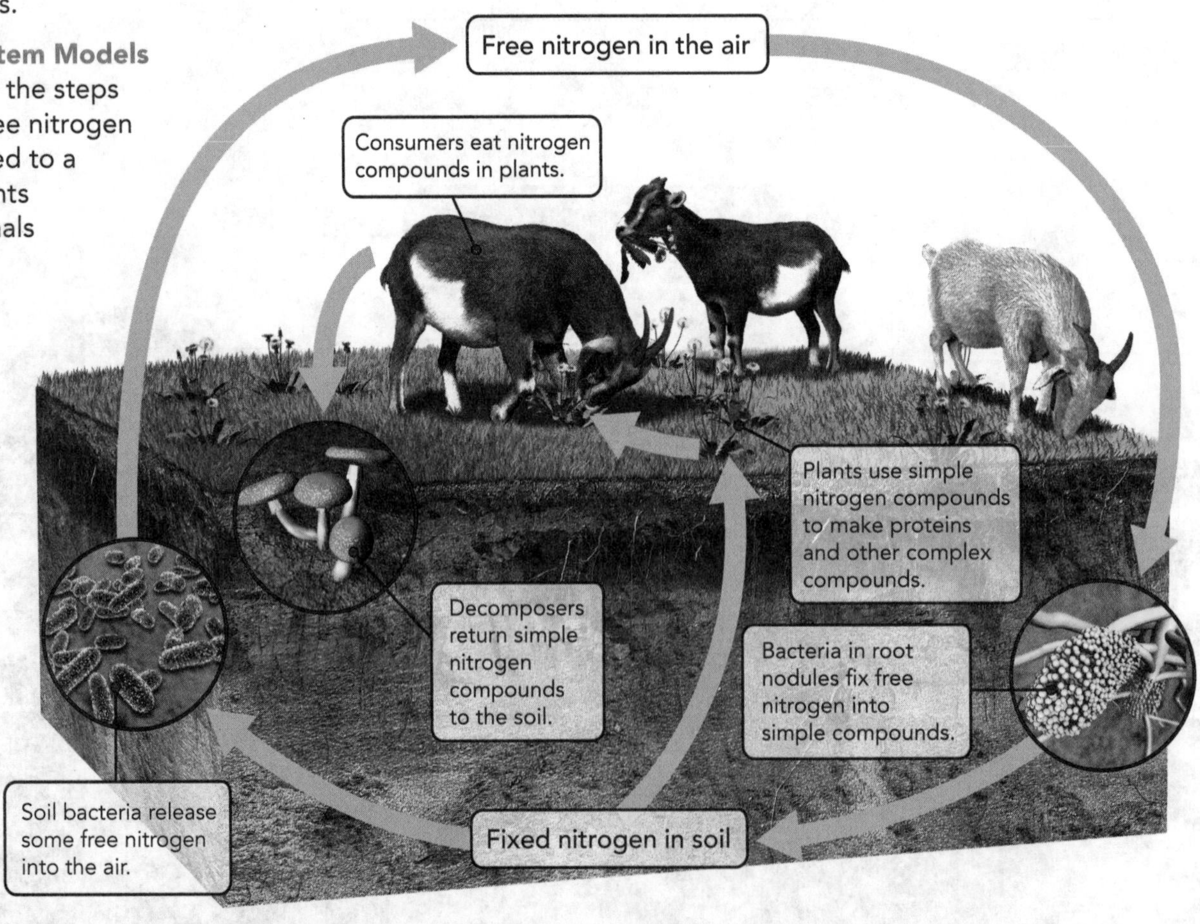

Recycling Free Nitrogen Once nitrogen has been fixed, producers can use it to build proteins and other complex molecules. Nitrogen can cycle from the soil to producers and then to consumers many times. At some point, however, bacteria break down the nitrogen compounds into free nitrogen. The free nitrogen rises back into the air and the cycle begins again. This is also an example of the Law of Conservation of Mass. Throughout the cycling of nitrogen, the number of atoms remains constant. Nitrogen atoms may take the form of gas (free nitrogen) or they may take the form of nitrogen-containing compounds, but the atoms are never created or destroyed.

READING CHECK **Summarize Text** Why is nitrogen fixation necessary?

....

Dependent and Independent Variables

Soybean plants are legumes that host nitrogen-fixing bacteria in their root nodules. Researchers wanted to know whether the plants would produce more seeds if nitrogen-fixing bacteria called *Rhizobia* were added to the soil during planting. The graph below shows the results of the experiment.

1. **Analyze Relationships** Underline the independent variable and circle the dependent variable in the graph. Then explain their relationship.

....

....

2. **CCC Use Mathematics** Write an equation that represents the difference in seed yield between beans without treatment and beans with treatment.

....

....

....

....

....

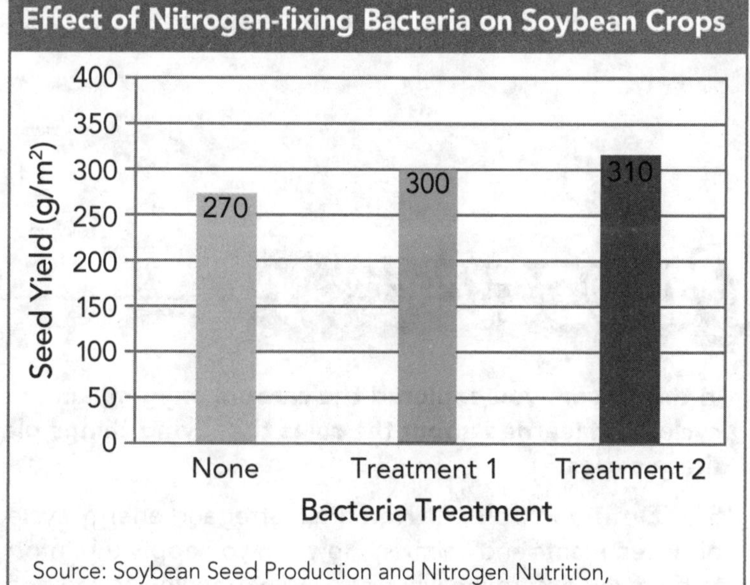

Source: Soybean Seed Production and Nitrogen Nutrition, A Comprehensive Survey of International Soybean Research (2013)

3. **SEP Interpret Data** Did the bacterial treatment have any effect? Use evidence from the graph to support your answer.

....

....

....

LESSON 3 Check

MS-LS2-3

1. CCC Systems What are the two roles of bacteria in the nitrogen cycle?

2. SEP Construct Explanations How does water get up to the atmosphere, and how does it get back down to Earth's surface?

3. SEP Develop Models Sketch and label a diagram in the space below showing how carbon cycles through an ecosystem.

4. CCC Energy and Matter What is the Law of Conservation of Mass? Why is it important in Earth's recycling of water, oxygen, carbon, and nitrogen. Give one example.

5. CCC Energy and Matter Compare the cycling of water and nutrients through an ecosystem to the cycling of blood in your cardiovascular system. What is the source of energy in each case?

Quest CHECK-IN

In this lesson, you explored the carbon, oxygen, and nitrogen cycles and learned about the roles that living things play in these cycles.

SEP Define Problems How are matter and energy cycled between plants and animals? How can you apply this information to help you determine what is going happening to the pond?

INTERACTIVITY

Matter and Energy in a Pond

Go online to to investigate how matter and energy are cycled in a pond ecosystem.

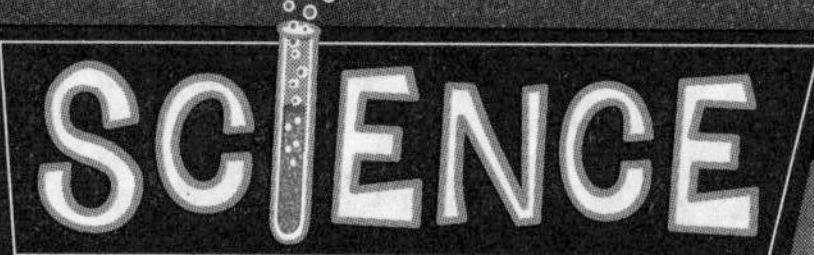

MS-LS2-1, MS-LS2-3

An Appetite for Plastic?!

Organic materials, such as bone and leaves, get cycled through ecosystems by decomposers. Materials like rock and metal break down more slowly. Plastics, however, are manufactured products that cannot be broken down easily. Additionally, they are problematic for the environment. Scientists have been trying for decades to discover a way to degrade plastic. Now, it seems they may have found an answer inside the guts of two tiny larvae.

Wax worms live in beehives where they feed off beeswax. What is bad for bees, may be good for people who are looking for a way to deal with Earth's plastic problem. Scientists have found out that wax worms can digest plastic bags! How they do this isn't clear yet. It may be that bacteria living in the wax worm's gut allow it to break down the plastic. Another possibility is that the wax worm produces an enzyme, a substance that speeds up reactions in an organism's body, that helps it degrade the plastic.

Wax worms aren't the only ones getting attention for their eating habits! Mealworms are the larvae of a species of beetle. They are fed to pet reptiles, fish, and birds. Scientists have observed that mealworms can break down plastic foam, such as the kind used in coffee cups and packing materials.

Scientists are trying to figure out how these larvae are able to degrade plastic. It may be a long time before we figure out how to use that knowledge on a scale large enough to reduce global plastic pollution.

MY-DISCOVERY

Use the Internet or other sources to investigate how wax worms and mealworms are able to break down different types of plastics. Create a chart that shows what type of plastic each larva can eat and how its body is able to break down plastic.

Mealworms are able to break down plastic foam.

A wax worm can munch its way through through this plastic shopping bag.

TOPIC 2 Review and Assess

1 Living Things and the Environment

MS-LS2-1

1. Which of the following describes a population?
   A. 85 great white sharks off Cape Cod
   B. thousands of dolphins and whales around Hawaii
   C. a mating pair of seagulls migrating to an island
   D. corals, sponges, algae, reef fish, lobsters, and giant clams

2. Which of the following is a biotic factor that might limit a population of mice?
   A. water for the mice to drink
   B. rainy weather that floods the mice's nests
   C. owls that prey on the mice
   D. rocks in which the mice can hide from predators

3. In terms of its effect on population, which factor is most similar to birth rate?
   A. immigration B. density
   C. emigration D. carrying capacity

4. **Apply Concepts** Name two biotic and two abiotic factors you might find in a desert ecosystem.

5. **SEP Construct Explanations** Describe how the availability of water can limit the growth of a population that otherwise has unlimited resources.

2 Energy Flow in Ecosystems

MS-LS2-3

6. Which of the following terms describes a straight series of connections among organisms that feed on each other?
   A. food web B. ecosystem
   C. community D. food chain

7. Mushrooms and bacteria are important
   A. predators. B. decomposers.
   C. producers. D. herbivores.

8. **CCC System Models** What does an energy pyramid show?

9. **SEP Develop Models** Draw a food web to illustrate the relationships among grass, a grasshopper, a mouse, a rabbit, a coyote, and hawk. Use the following information:
   - grass is a producer
   - a grasshopper is a first-level consumer
   - a mouse and a rabbit are first- and second-level consumers
   - a coyote is a second- and third-level consumer
   - a hawk is a third-level consumer

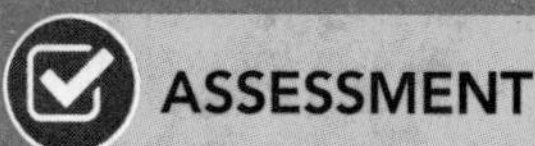

Evaluate your understanding by taking a Topic Test.

3 Cycles of Matter

MS-LS2-3

10. **Distinguish Relationships** What is different about how producers and consumers get energy?

....

11. **Determine Similarities** In terms of how they get energy, are decomposers more like producers or consumers? Explain.

....

12. **Consider Limitations** In your opinion, is a food web or a food chain a more accurate representation of how energy and matter flow in an ecosystem? Explain.

....

13. What do consumers release as they break down food to obtain energy?
    A. sugar
    B. carbon dioxide and water
    C. free nitrogen
    D. oxygen

14. Rain, hail, and snow are all examples of
    A. condensation. B. evaporation.
    C. erosion. D. precipitation.

15. In one form of nitrogen fixation, the .... energy of .... splits nitrogen molecules into atoms.
    A. chemical, water vapor
    B. mechanical, consumers
    C. electrical, lightning
    D. released, bacteria

16. **SEP Use Evidence** Cite evidence to show that living systems follow the Laws of Conservation of Mass and Energy.

....

17. **CCC Energy and Matter** How is carbon cycled between organisms and the environment?

....

TOPIC 2 Review and Assess

MS-LS2-3

Evidence-Based Assessment

A team of field biologists is studying energy roles and relationships among organisms in a tropical rainforest habitat in Southeast Asia. One of the biologists diagrams some of these relationships in a food web.

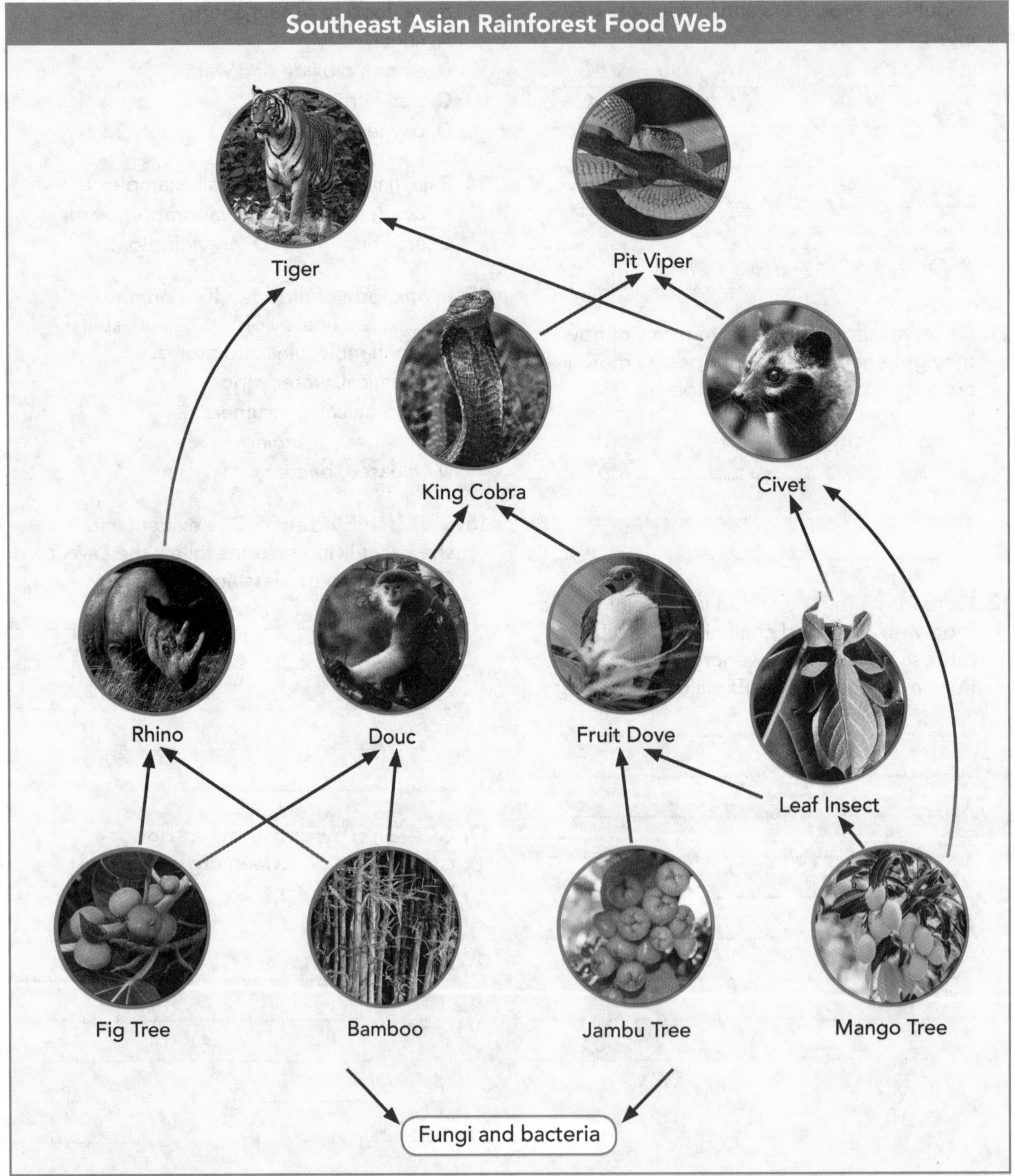

1. SEP Use Models Which organism from the food web is a producer?

A. bamboo
B. civet
C. douc
D. tiger

2. CCC Energy and Matter Why are there only two organisms, the tiger and pit viper, at the top level of this food web?

3. CCC System Models Explain the role of decomposers in cycling of matter between the living and nonliving parts of the Southeast Asian rainforest ecosystem.

4. CCC Stability and Change If the fruit dove were removed from the food web, how would it impact the Southeast Asian rainforest ecosystem?

5. SEP Construct Arguments As matter is cycled and energy flows through this system, how are both conserved? Use details from the food web to support your response.

Quest FINDINGS

Complete the Quest!

Phenomenon Identify what you believe is the cause of the algal bloom at Pleasant Pond, and describe the impact it has had on the organisms in this ecosystem. Include a proposal about restoring the pond using evidence from your investigation.

CCC Cause and Effect What is the connection between the water in Pleasant Pond—an abiotic factor—and the biotic factors?

INTERACTIVITY

Reflections on a Pond

uDemonstrate Lab

MS-LS2-1, MS-LS2-3

Last Remains

How can you **confirm** an owl's role in a **food web**?

Background

Phenomenon Your community has a rodent problem! Squirrels and mice seem to be taking over. Some members of your community have suggested that introducing more barn owls into the neighborhood will bring the rodent population under control. But people want to be sure that barn owls do hunt and eat mice and squirrels before they go to the trouble of introducing these nocturnal birds to the community.

You will design and carry out an investigation by observing remains found in an owl pellet—undigested material an owl spits up. You will relate your findings to food webs and energy flow in the owl's ecosystem. Using the evidence you have collected, you will confirm whether or not the idea to introduce more barn owls into your community will help to bring the rodent population under control.

(per group)

- goggles, 2 pairs
- gloves, 2 pairs
- owl pellet, 1 per group
- probes, 2
- tweezers, 1 per group
- hand lens
- paper towels
- bone identification charts

Be sure to follow all safety guidelines provided by your teacher. The Safety Appendix of your textbook provides more details about the safety icons.

House mouse

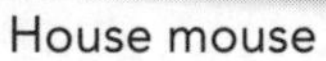

Gray squirrel

Design Your Investigation

☐ 1. Your investigation will involve observing an owl pellet, which is regurgitated or "spit up" remains of food. Owls generally eat their prey whole and then get rid of the parts of the organisms that they cannot digest, such as bones and fur.

☐ 2. Develop a procedure for your investigation. Consider the following questions to help develop your plan:
- How will you use the materials provided by your teacher?
- What observations will you make?
- How will you use the remains in the pellet to determine what the owl eats?
- How can you use the bone identification charts to help you identify the remains of organisms?

☐ 3. Write the procedure for your investigation in the space provided.

☐ 4. Create a data table to record your observations. Include whether each organism you find inside the owl pellet is a herbivore, a carnivore, or an omnivore.

☐ 5. After receiving your teacher's approval for the procedure you developed, carry out your investigation.

HANDS-ON LAB

Demonstrate Go online for a downloadable worksheet of this lab.

Procedure

Data Table and Observations

Analyze and Interpret Data

1. **SEP Develop Models** Diagram the cycling of matter and energy in the barn owl's habitat. Begin by drawing a food chain. Then develop the food chain into a simple food web using additional organisms that you might find in the habitat. Include captions for your diagram that explain the cycling matter and flow of energy among the organisms.

2. **Claim** Do you think the introduction of more barn owls into your community will solve your mouse and squirrel problem? Use evidence from your investigation to support your response.

3. **Evidence** What information did you find out by observing the remains in the owl pellet?

4. **Reasoning** Owls hunt at night. Using your findings from the owl pellet, what conclusions can you draw about whether squirrels and mice are more active during the day or at night?

TOPIC 3

Populations, Communities, and Ecosystems

NGSS PERFORMANCE EXPECTATIONS

MS-LS2-1 Analyze and interpret data to provide evidence for the effects of resource availability on organisms and populations of organisms in an ecosystem.

MS-LS2-2 Construct an explanation that predicts patterns of interactions among organisms across multiple ecosystems.

MS-LS2-3 Develop a model to describe the cycling of matter and flow of energy among living and nonliving parts of an ecosystem.

MS-LS2-4 Construct an argument supported by empirical evidence that changes to physical or biological components of an ecosystem affect populations.

MS-LS2-5 Evaluate competing design solutions for maintaining biodiversity and ecosystem services.

HANDS-ON LAB

uConnect Explore how communities change in response to natural disasters.

GO ONLINE
to access your digital course

VIDEO

INTERACTIVITY

VIRTUAL LAB

ASSESSMENT

eTEXT

HANDS-ON LABS

Why would these deer risk crossing a busy road?

The Essential Question
How do living and nonliving things affect one another?

SEP Construct Explanations Crossing a road can be dangerous business. What might the deer be trying to get to on the other side of the road that makes it worth the risk? List some living and nonliving resources that the road makes it difficult for the deer to get to.

....

....

....

....

....

....

Quest KICKOFF

Should an Animal Crossing Be Constructed in My Community?

Phenomenon A company wants to build a new factory nearby, but wants the state to build a new highway to the location. The highway would allow employees and products to access the site. However, the highway would pass through an area with endangered species. Before the state decides, they contact a wildlife biologist to study the impact the highway would have on the local ecosystem. In this problem-based Quest activity, you will investigate how the construction of highways can affect organisms. By applying what you learn in each lesson, in a digital activity or hands-on lab, you will gather key Quest information and evidence. With the information, you will propose a solution in the Findings activity.

INTERACTIVITY
To Cross or Not to Cross

MS-LS2-5 Evaluate competing design solutions for maintaining biodiversity and ecosystem services.

After watching the Quest kickoff video, where a wildlife biologist discusses animal crossings in Banff National Park, fill in the 3-2-1 activity.

3 organisms I think are at risk locally

....

....

....

2 ideas I have to help them

....

....

....

1 thing I learned from the wildlife biologist

....

....

Quest CHECK-IN

IN LESSON 1

How do animal crossings effect ecosystems? Analyze some effects then brainstorm ideas for your animal crossing and identify the criteria and constraints you need to consider.

INTERACTIVITY
Research Animal Crossings

Quest CHECK-IN

IN LESSON 2

How does community stakeholder feedback impact your design ideas, criteria, and constraints? Evaluate your design.

INTERACTIVITY
Community Opinions

Quest CHECK-IN

IN LESSON 3

STEM What are the criteria and constraints for the animal crossing? Evaluate competing design solutions.

HANDS-ON LAB
Design and Model a Crossing

This crossing over the highway looks like it is part of the surrounding forest. It's a much safer route for the animals, and keeps the drivers who pass underneath safe as well.

IN LESSON 4

How could a highway affect local ecosystem services? Consider your animal crossing design and how it might also affect ecosystem services.

Quest FINDINGS

Complete the Quest!

Determine the best way to clearly present your claim with data and evidence, such as graphics or a multimedia presentation.

INTERACTIVITY

Reflect on Your Animal Crossing

uConnect Lab

MS-LS2-2, MS-LS2-4

How Communities Change

How can you **interpret data** to infer how changes to ecosystems will affect populations?

Materials

(per group)

- photos provided by teacher

Background

Phenomenon Think about how the area in which you live changes. All communities change over time. When natural disasters occur, communities change quickly.

Use a Model

☐ **1.** What categories of data can you collect about how an area has changed? Then, look at the photos and record the specific changes that you observe in the table.

....

....

☐ **2.** Next study the illustrations of primary succession. Collect the same type of data you described in step 1.

Observations

uConnect Go online for a downloadable worksheet of this lab.

Changes in a Neighborhood

Succession in an Ecosystem

Analyze and Conclude

1. **Connect to the Environment** How were changes in the human-built environment similar to changes in the natural ecosystem? How were they different?

2. **CCC Cause and Effect** What types of disruptions could take place in the ecosystem that would affect the populations of organisms that live there?

3. **SEP Cite Evidence** How do you think earlier organisms make it possible for later species to live in that ecosystem? Use evidence to support your answer.

LESSON 1

Interactions in Ecosystems

Guiding Questions

- How can resource availability affect interactions between organisms?
- How is population size affected by predation and symbiotic relationships?
- How are patterns of interactions between organisms similar in different ecosystems?

Connections

Literacy Determine Central Ideas

Math Construct Graphs

MS-LS2-1, MS-LS2-2

HANDS-ON LAB

uInvestigate Model competition between organisms.

Vocabulary

niche
competition
predation
symbiosis
commensalism
mutualism
parasitism

Academic Vocabulary

interactions

Connect It!

Outline the hidden insect in the image. What adaptations do you notice?

SEP Construct Explanations How do the animal's adaptations help it survive?

....

....

CCC Cause and Effect How does your body adapt to its environment?

....

....

....

....

Adaptations and Survival

Each organism in an ecosystem has special characteristics. These characteristics influence whether an individual can survive and reproduce in its environment. A characteristic that makes an individual better suited to a specific environment may eventually become common in that species through a process called natural selection.

In this process, individuals with characteristics that are well-suited to a particular environment tend to survive and produce more offspring. Offspring inheriting these characteristics also are more likely to survive to reproduce. Natural selection results in adaptations—the behaviors and physical characteristics that allow organisms to live successfully in their environments. As an example, a great white shark's body is white along its underside, but dark across the top. The shark blends with the surroundings in the water whether being looked at from below or above. **Figure 1** shows another example of how a species adapts to its environment.

Individuals with characteristics that do not help them survive in their environments are less likely to reproduce. Over time, these unhelpful characteristics may affect the survival of a species. If individuals in a species cannot adapt successfully to changes in their environment, the species can become extinct.

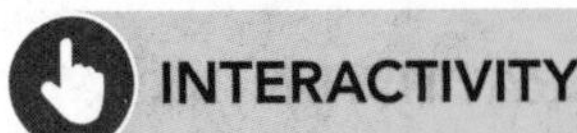

Identify competition in your daily life.

Reflect In what ways have organisms in your local area adapted to the environment? In your science notebook, describe characteristics that make the organism successful.

Adaptation and Survival

Figure 1 Different kinds of adaptations work together to aid survival.

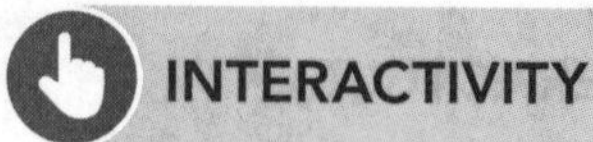
INTERACTIVITY

Model what competition looks like in nature.

Niche The organisms in any ecosystem have adaptations that help them fill specific roles or functions. The role of an organism in its habitat is called its niche. A **niche** includes how an organism obtains its food, the type of food the organism eats, and what other organisms eat it.

Remember that an organism's energy role in an ecosystem is determined by how it obtains food and how it interacts with other organisms. Adaptations by a species allow a population to live successfully on the available resources in its niche. Abiotic factors also influence a population's ability to survive in the niche it occupies. Lack of water or space, for example, may cause a population to decline and no longer fit well into that niche. Biotic factors, such as predators or a reduced food source, affect the populations in a niche and may change an organism's ability to survive.

A niche also includes when and how the organism reproduces and the physical conditions it requires to survive. Every organism has a variety of adaptations that suit it to specific living conditions and help it survive. Use **Figure 2** to describe characteristics of a giraffe's niche.

Niche Characteristics

Figure 2 This picture shows that organisms occupy many niches in an environment.

A Safari Guide's Q & A

I observed this giraffe in the wild during a group safari. Here are some questions I received. Can you answer them?

Relate Text to Visuals What does the feeding behavior of the giraffe tell you about its niche?

....

....

READING CHECK **Determine Central Ideas** What adaptations might the giraffe have that help it survive in its environment?

....

....

Egret Wades into water to grab small fish.
Flamingo Feeds on tiny organisms on the muddy bottom.
Oystercatcher Uses its narrow beak to pry open shellfish.
Skimmer Nabs small fish on the surface of the water.

Shorebird Competition

Figure 3 ✏ Draw a line from each bird to the location where it feeds.

Competition and Predation

In every type of ecosystem, a range of **interactions** takes place among organisms every day. Two major types of interactions among organisms are competition and predation.

Competition More than one species of organism can live in the same habitat and obtain the same food. For example, in a desert ecosystem, a flycatcher and an elf owl both live on the saguaro cactus and eat insects. However, these two species do not occupy exactly the same niche. The flycatcher is active during the day, while the owl is active mostly at night.

When two species share a niche, one of their populations might be affected. The reason for this is **competition**. The struggle between organisms to survive as they use the same limited resources is called competition. For example, different species of birds in a park compete for the same bugs and worms to eat. If one population of birds is more successful, it will increase while the other population decreases.

In any ecosystem, there are limited amounts of food, water, and shelter. Organisms that share the same habitat often have adaptations that enable them to reduce competition. Observe the shorebirds in **Figure 3** and discover how their niches vary in the shoreline habitat.

Academic Vocabulary

How have you heard the term *interactions* used in another subject and what does the word mean in that context?

....

....

....

....

....

Investigate Model competition between organisms.

Predation A tiger shark bursts through the water and grabs a sea snake swimming on the surface. An interaction in which one organism kills another for food or nutrients is called **predation**. In this interaction, one organism is the predator and the other is the prey. The tiger shark, for example, is the predator and the sea snake is the prey. These interactions happen throughout nature. Predator and prey interactions may reduce the number of organisms or eliminate the populations.

Adaptations All species have ways of supporting their survival in their environment. Some predators have adaptations, such as sharp teeth and claws, well-developed senses, and the ability to run fast, which help them to catch and kill their prey. Prey organisms may have protective coverings, warning coloration, or the ability to camouflage themselves to help them avoid being killed. Study the predator-prey interaction in **Figure 4.**

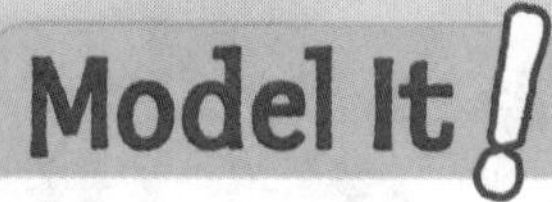

Predator and Prey Adaptations

Figure 4 In a rainforest ecosystem, a gecko finds out that the flexible snake can hold onto tree bark with its muscles and scales as it hunts.

SEP Develop Models Consider a grassland ecosystem of tall, tan savanna grasses. Draw either a predator or a prey organism that might live there. Label the adaptations that will allow your organism to be successful.

Population Size Predation affects population size. Changes in population size occur when new members arrive or when members leave. Population size increases if more members enter than leave, and declines if more members leave than arrive. Too many predators in a area can decrease the prey population, leading to less food availability and possible predator population decline. In general, predator and prey populations rise and fall together in predictable patterns.

☑ READING CHECK **Summarize** What effect do competition and predation have on population size?

....

....

Math Toolbox

Predator-Prey Interactions

Moose and Wolf

Populations on Isle Royale

On Isle Royale, an island in Lake Superior, the populations of wolves (the predator) and moose (the prey) rise and fall in cycles.

Year	Wolves	Moose
1985	22	976
1990	15	1,315
1995	16	2,117
2000	29	2,007
2005	30	540
2010	19	510
2015	2	1,300

1. **Construct Graphs** Create a double line graph of the data above. Fill in the x-axis and both y-axes. Use a different color line for each animal and provide a key.

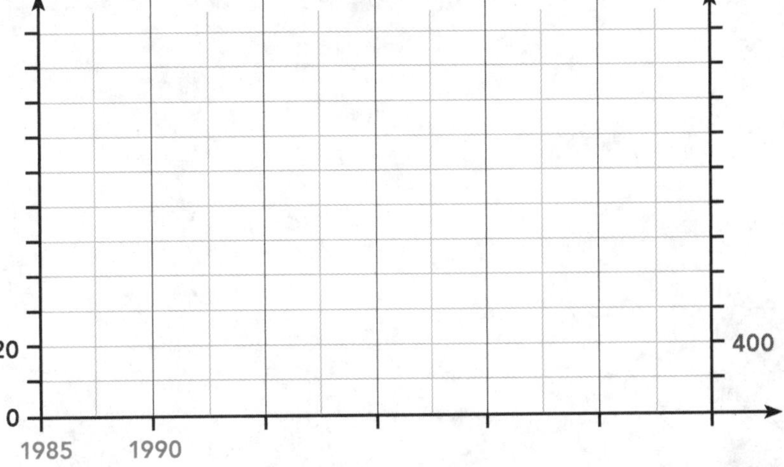

2. **Analyze and Interpret Data** Describe the relationship shown by your graph and suggest factors that impact it.

....

....

....

....

....

INTERACTIVITY

Classify symbiotic relationships.

VIDEO

Explore the three types of symbiotic relationships.

Literacy Connection

Determine Central Ideas As you read, determine the central idea of the text. Note how this idea is developed through examples. Underline examples that you think most clearly explain the central idea.

Symbiotic Relationships

Symbiosis is a third type of interaction among organisms. **Symbiosis** (sim bee OH sis) is any relationship in which two species live closely together. There are three types of symbiotic relationships: commensalism, mutualism, and parasitism.

Commensalism Birds build nests in trees to make a place to live. The tree is unharmed. This relationship is an example of **commensalism**. Commensalism (kuh MEN suh liz um) is a relationship in which one species benefits and the other species is neither helped nor harmed.

Mutualism In some interactions, two species may depend on one another. In Africa, oxpecker birds and zebras display this relationship. The oxpecker bird rides on the zebra's back, eating bugs that crawl on the animal. The bird gets a meal and the zebra has harmful pests removed. This relationship is an example of **mutualism** (MYOO choo uh liz um), which is a relationship in which both species benefit.

Commensalism is not very common in nature because two species are usually either helped or harmed a little by any interaction. Scientists may disagree on whether a particular relationship truly demonstrates commensalism.

For example, clownfish live among the poisonous and stinging tentacles of sea anemones to avoid being eaten by larger fish. Some scientists think that the relationship between clownfish and sea anemones is commensalism, while others think the sea anemones also benefit from this relationship, making it an example of mutualism. Identifying examples of commensalism can be difficult. See examples of some of these relationships in **Figure 5**.

Mutualism and Commensalism

Figure 5 Some relationships more clearly show benefits to one or both species than others.

1. Synthesize Information ✏ Read each image caption. Label each photo "M" for mutualism or "C" for commensalism in the circle provided.
2. SEP Cite Evidence ✏ Beneath each image, use evidence to justify how you classified the relationship.

Hummingbirds feed on nectar deep within a flower. While the bird sips, the flower's pollen rubs off on the hummingbird. The bird can carry it to another flower.

SEP Evidence ....

....

....

The banded mongoose feeds on ticks and other tiny animals that nestle in the warthog's fur and feed off of the warthog.

SEP Evidence ....

....

....

....

Barnacles feed by filtering tiny organisms from the water. They grow on objects below the surface, such as piers and rocks, and attach themselves to whales.

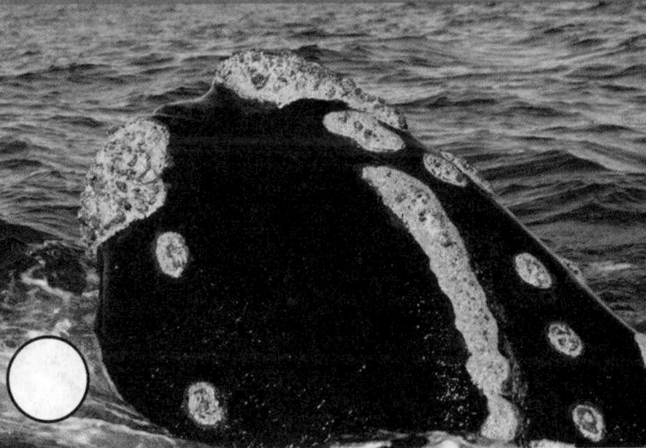

SEP Evidence ....

....

....

....

Remora attach themselves to the underside of a manta ray with a suction-cup-like structure. Mantas are messy eaters and remora feed on the food scraps.

SEP Evidence ....

....

....

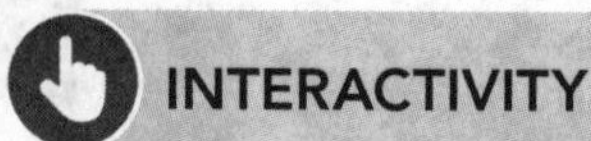

INTERACTIVITY

Interpret models of relationships in different ecosystems.

Parasitism If you've ever seen a dog continually scratching itself, then it may have fleas. This interaction is an example of **parasitism** (PAHR uh sit iz um). Parasitism is a relationship that involves one organism living with, on, or inside another organism and harming it.

The organism that benefits is called a parasite. The host is the organism that the parasite lives in or on. The parasite is generally smaller than its host. The fleas, for example, are parasites that harm the dog by biting it to feed on its blood for nourishment. Pets can suffer from severe health problems as a result of these bites. Study the examples of parasitism in **Figure 6**.

Parasitic Relationships

Figure 6 Unlike a predator, a parasite does not usually kill the organism it feeds on. If the host dies, the parasite could lose its source of food or shelter.

READING CHECK **Integrate with Visuals** In each picture, label the host and the parasite shown.

SEP Construct Explanations How does parasitism differ from other symbiotic relationships?

....

....

....

....

....

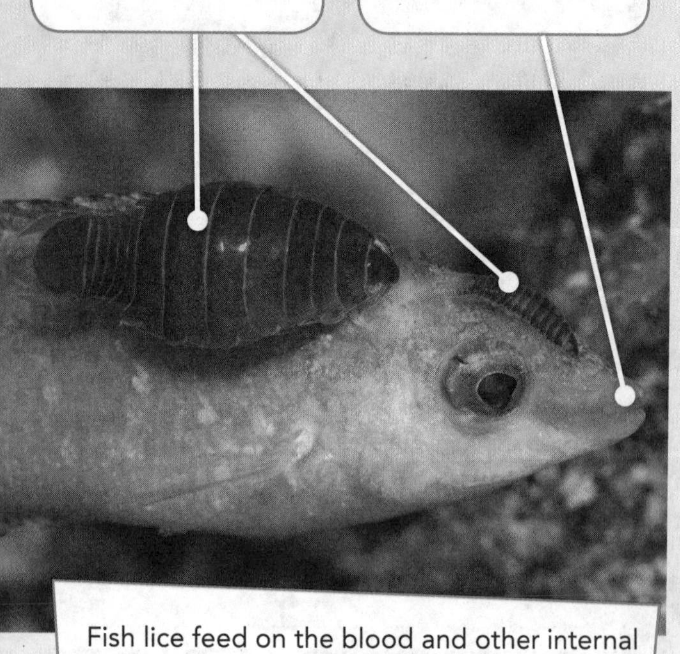

Fish lice feed on the blood and other internal fluids of the fish. Eventually the fish may quit eating and lose color from the stress caused by the lice.

A braconid wasp lays its eggs under the skin of the tomato hornworm. After the larvae emerge, they form cocoons on the hornworm. As the larvae develop inside the cocoons, they feed on the insides of the hornworm.

LESSON 1 Check

MS-LS2-1, MS-LS2-2

1. **Identify** What are the five different types of interactions between organisms?

Use the graph you constructed on wolf and moose populations to help you answer Questions 2 and 3.

2. **CCC Patterns** What patterns do scientists observe between predator-prey relationships like the wolves and moose on Isle Royale?

3. **SEP Interpret Data** Use the data from your graph to provide evidence for the effects of resource availability on individuals and populations in an ecosystem.

4. **SEP Construct Explanations** Do the patterns of interactions between organisms, such as competition and predation, change when they occur in different ecosystems?

5. **CCC Cause and Effect** Predict the effects on a predator-prey relationship, such as the one between a frog and blue heron, in a wetland ecosystem in the midst of a drought.

Quest CHECK-IN

In this lesson, you learned how organisms in ecosystems interact with one another and how resource availability can affect these interactions. You also discovered that these interactions can influence population size.

CCC Analyze Systems Why is it important to maintain existing organism interactions and availability of resources when building a new highway?

INTERACTIVITY

Research Animal Crossings

Go online to investigate the effects of highways and animals crossings.

LESSON

Dynamic and Resilient Ecosystems

Guiding Questions

- How can changes to physical or biological components of an ecosystem affect organisms and populations?
- How do natural events impact the environment?
- How do human activities impact ecosystems?

Connection

Literacy Write Arguments

MS-LS2-1, MS-LS2-2, MS-LS2-4

HANDS-ON LAB

uInvestigate Identify examples of succession in a local ecosystem.

Vocabulary

succession
pioneer species

Academic Vocabulary

colonize
dominate

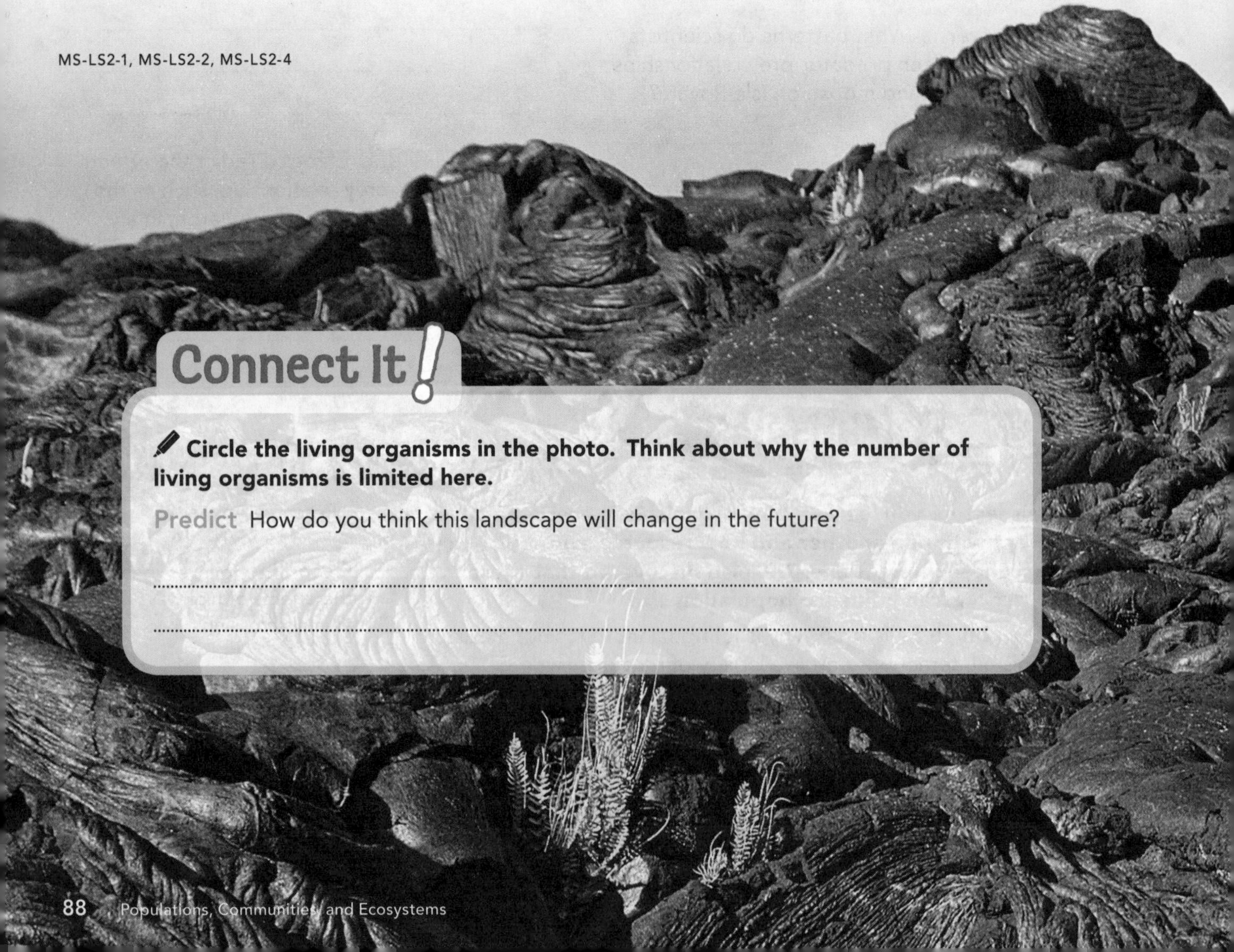

Connect It!

Circle the living organisms in the photo. Think about why the number of living organisms is limited here.

Predict How do you think this landscape will change in the future?

....

....

Succession

Ecosystems and their communities are always changing. Natural disasters, such as floods and tornadoes, can cause rapid change. Other changes occur over centuries or even longer. Humans can have a major impact on ecosystems as well. The series of predictable changes that occur in a community over time is called **succession**. As you can see in **Figure 1**, organisms can establish habitats in even the harshest environments.

Primary Succession Disruptions to the physical or biological components of an ecosystem can impact organism populations living there. For example, lava from a volcanic eruption is creating new land by the sea. When the lava cools and hardens, no organisms are present. Over time, living things will **colonize** these areas. Primary succession is the series of changes that occur in an area where no soil or organisms exist.

Pioneer Species The first species to populate an area are called **pioneer species.** These species are usually mosses and lichens, carried to the area by wind or water. Lichens are fungi and algae growing in a symbiotic relationship. They give off acidic compounds that help dissolve rock into soil. As pioneer species die, their remains add nutrients to the thin soil and help build it up.

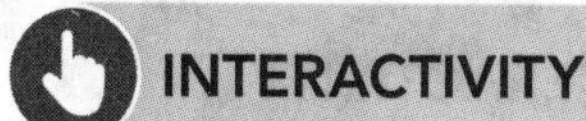

Consider what happens when an ecosystem is disturbed.

Academic Vocabulary

Where else have you heard the term *colonize*, or the related term *colony*? Provide an example.

....

....

....

....

Succession

Figure 1 Harsh landscapes like this hardened lava flow transform over time as lichens and plants establish themselves.

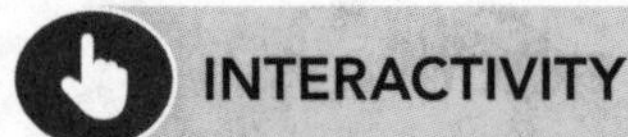

INTERACTIVITY

Investigate how ecosystems can change over time.

Literacy Connection

Write Arguments Write a letter to a local government official explaining the importance of preventing disruptions to mature communities. In your letter, include evidence to support your claim.

Mature Communities Small changes in one part of a system can cause large changes in another part. For example, because lichens help to form a thin layer of soil, seed-producing plants can then establish themselves. Wind, water, and birds can bring seeds into the area. If the soil is adequate and there's enough rainfall, seedlings will emerge and may grow to adulthood. As the plants grow, they will shed leaves that will break down to make more soil. Plants also attract animals that will further enhance the soil by leaving waste and their own remains. Over time, the buildup of organic matter will improve the soil and allow for a more diverse community to establish itself in the area.

Succession demonstrates how all natural systems go through cycles and processes that are required for their functioning. While it can take centuries for a community to mature, once a community is established it can last for thousands of years or more if it is not disturbed or disrupted.

Ecosystem Disruption

Figure 2 In 2017, wildfires raged through California's drought-stricken regions.

Secondary Succession Devastating fires, such as the one shown in **Figure 2**, can result from natural system processes or human activities. Regardless of their cause, fires lead to secondary succession. Secondary succession is the series of changes that occur in an area where the ecosystem has been disturbed, but where soil and organisms already exist. Natural disruptions that affect the physical and biological components of an ecosystem include fires, hurricanes, tsunamis, and tornadoes. Human activities may also disturb an ecosystem and cause secondary succession to occur.

Unlike primary succession (**Figure 3**), secondary succession occurs in a place where an ecosystem and community exist. Secondary succession usually occurs more rapidly than primary succession because soil is already present and seeds from some plants may remain in the soil. Over time, more and more organisms can live in the area and it starts to resemble places that were never disturbed in the first place.

Empirical evidence is what's based on experience or verified by observation. Scientists follow common rules for obtaining and evaluating empirical evidence. What we know about succession in natural ecosystems is based on both empirical evidence and on data that has been gathered and analyzed over years and even decades.

READING CHECK **Cite Textual Evidence** How is secondary succession different from primary succession?

....

....

....

Model It

Pioneers

Figure 3 The images show how pioneer species begin the process of succession, which changes an area over time.

Integrate Information Draw pictures to represent the missing stages of primary succession.

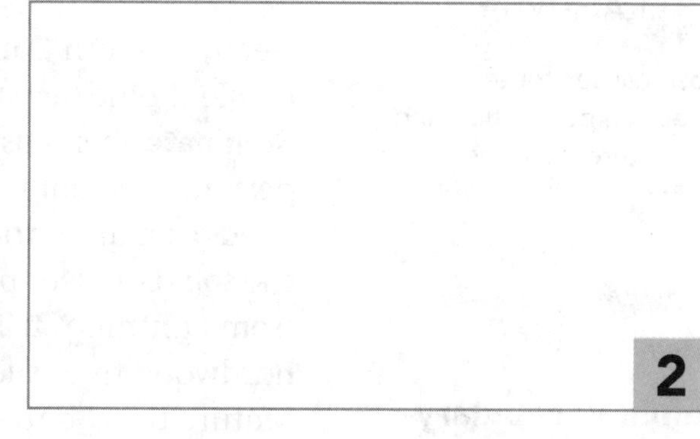

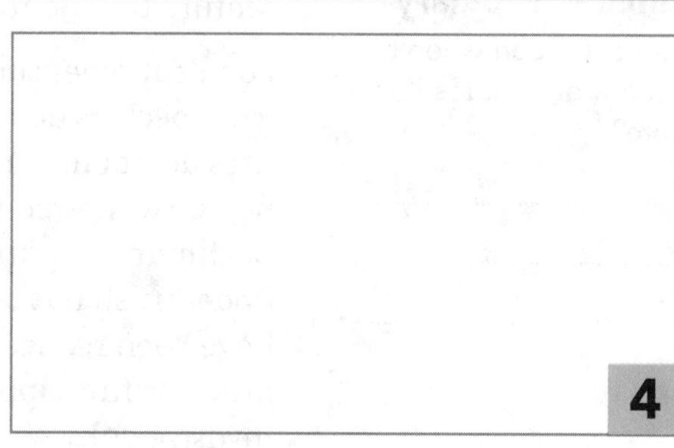

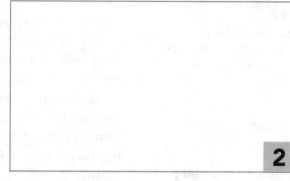

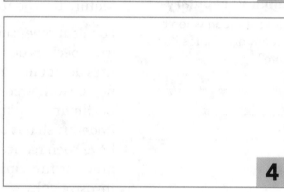

1. **Claim** Identify a place in your community where succession might occur if people abandoned the area.

   ....

2. **Evidence** Describe what the location would look like years later after being abandoned.

   ....

   ....

   ....

3. **Reasoning** Explain how changes to the physical and biological components of the ecosystem would affect the populations that make up the community.

   ....

   ....

   ....

   ....

   ....

Investigate Identify examples of succession in a local ecosystem.

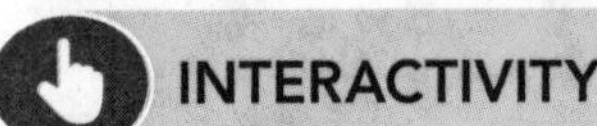

Propose causes for a changes in a population and predict future changes.

Academic Vocabulary

What does it mean when a sports team *dominates* its rival team?

Ecosystem Disruptions and Population Survival

When changes to physical and biological components occur rapidly or lastingly, most populations in the ecosystem do not survive. However, some organisms do survive the changes. Organisms surviving a fast-changing ecosystem often have adaptations that help them thrive in the new conditions.

Georgia, South Carolina, and Florida have an ecosystem of the longleaf pine forest, as shown in **Figure 4.** Longleaf pine trees **dominate** this ecosystem. These trees grow in a pattern that permits sunlight to reach the forest floor. Longleaf pine seeds need a soil free from undergrowth and germinate quickly in the soil. Longleaf pines are dependent on regular forest fires from lightning strikes to burn away grasses and invasive hardwood trees such as oak to remain healthy and reproduce. Mature trees' bark and early growth are fire-resistant.

Longleaf pines support a healthy ecosystem. Red-cockaded woodpeckers depend on mature trees for nesting sites. If fires don't burn the undergrowth, predators can reach the nests. Swallowed-tailed kites build nests high in the trees. Bachmann's sparrows favor mature pine forests where underbrush has been removed by fires. These bird populations have been reduced due to logging of the longleaf pines and previous fire suppression practices, which opened space for invasive oaks.

Most organisms reappear at some point after the fire because of adaptations such as heat-resistant seeds that may sprout or underground roots that can grow. Young longleaf pines develop a long taproot that enables them to grow after a fire.

Changes to Populations

Figure 4 In the longleaf pine ecosystem, some organisms are adapted to survive fire and others are not.

READING CHECK **Determine Central Ideas** How does a wildfire impact a population of oak trees?

CCC Cause and Effect How might a wildfire help the longleaf pine population survive a deadly fungal infection on the needles of seedlings?

The red-cockaded woodpecker flies away from the fire to safety.
As the thick, scaly bark burns, flakes fall off and take the heat with them.
A longleaf pine seedling is topped with a moist tuft of needles. As fire burns the needles, they produce steam that moves the heat away from the plant and extinguishes the fire. If the needles burn off entirely, the seedling can regrow from its root.
Fire burns the blades of bluestem grass, but its underground roots remain unharmed. After the fire, new shoots sprout from the roots.
The pine snake escapes fire by seeking shelter in a gopher burrow.

LESSON 2 Check

MS-LS2-1, MS-LS2-2, MS-LS2-4

1. SEP Construct Explanations What are pioneer species? How do they affect the variety of organisms in an ecosystem?

2. SEP Engage in Argument Support the argument that a forest fire impacts a population of birds that nest in the trees.

3. CCC Cause and Effect Explain how the physical and biological components of the ecosystem in the image are being disrupted.

Quest CHECK-IN

In this lesson you learned that changes to physical or biological components of an ecosystem can affect the populations of organisms that live there.

Apply Concepts How might mature communities of organisms be affected by the construction of a new highway? How does an animal crossing solve some of these problems?

INTERACTIVITY

Community Opinions

Go online to learn about reactions to a proposed crossing from members of the community. Based on the feedback, consider the constraints the animal crossing should meet.

MS-LS2-1, MS-LS2-2, MS-LS2-4

CAREERS

Field Biologist

Ecology in ACTION

Some biologists study the cells of living things. Others study living things as a whole. Field biologists study living things—along with their communities and ecosystems. Field biologists research the way all living things interact in an environment. Within this field, they may have a special focus on plants, animals, insects, soil, or many other subjects.

Some field biologists manage fisheries or work as pollution control technicians. Others might perform research on the environmental health of a specific plant, animal, or ecosystem. They might also be responsible for regulating and enforcing laws that protect the environment. Just as often, field biologists work for industries as environmentalists, monitoring the effects of an industry on its local environment. Field biologists may monitor any disruptions within parts of an ecosystem and determine how populations of organisms might be impacted.

To become a field biologist, you need to understand a wide range of sciences, including ecology, botany, zoology, marine biology, and ecosystem analysis. In the coming years, field biologists will study the long-term effects of certain industries on the environment. They will also analyze the effects of global warming on ecosystem interactions.

VIDEO

Field Biologist

MY CAREER

Type "field biologist" into an online search engine to learn more about this career.

Polar bears feed on seals that gather on and around slabs of sea ice. As sea ice shrinks, field biologists monitor how these animals are trying to adapt and how their populations are changing as a result.

LESSON

3 Biodiversity

GUIDING QUESTIONS

- What is the value of biodiversity?
- What factors affect biodiversity?
- How do human activities impact biodiversity?

Connections

Literacy Cite Textual Evidence

Math Use Ratio Reasoning

MS-LS2-4, MS-LS2-5, MS-LS4-1

HANDS-ON LAB

uInvestigate Explore the role of keystone species in maintaining biodiversity.

Vocabulary

biodiversity
keystone species
extinction
invasive species

Academic Vocabulary

value
economic

Connect It!

Circle the parts of the ecosystem shown here that you think are important to people.

Identify Unknowns What do you think are two important ways that humans benefit from a healthy ecosystem? Explain.

....

....

The Value of Biodiversity

Earth is filled with many different ecosystems that provide habitats for each and every organism. Some organisms live in one ecosystem their entire lives. Other organisms are born in one ecosystem and migrate to another. Healthy ecosystems have biodiversity. **Biodiversity** is the number and variety of different species in an area. Healthy ecosystems also provide the opportunity for different species to interact. This is often essential for their survival, such as a predator finding prey.

Changes in an ecosystem affect the species in that ecosystem. They are usually linked to available resources. Biodiversity increases as more resources are available. It decreases when fewer resources are available. When biodiversity changes, it impacts ecosystem processes. This impact may affect the health of an ecosystem.

Biodiversity also has both economic and ecological **value**. Healthy ecosystems, such as that in **Figure 1**, provide resources and materials that we use. We consume food, fuel, medicines, and fibers from healthy ecosystems.

Academic Vocabulary

What does it mean when someone says that a person was raised with good values? Provide two examples.

....

....

....

....

....

Healthy Ecosystems

Figure 1 Biodiversity determines the health of an ecosystem.

Academic Vocabulary

How would you explain the term *economic* to someone who did not understand the meaning?

Economic Value

Humans use ecosystems for our own profit. There is value in using ecosystems to fulfill our basic needs and wants. The products we take from ecosystems have **economic** value, such as providing a household income. People can profit from healthy ecosystems both directly or indirectly.

Resources that are consumed from an ecosystem provide a direct value. For example, the crops you see in **Figure 2** are direct value. The farmer used the land and grew the crops so that she can feed her family and make a profit on their sale. In addition to food, medicines and raw materials provide resources and income. Unfortunately, our demand for certain organisms and resources can harm biodiversity and ecosystems. Humans can use too many resources at once. As a result, many ecosystems do not have time to recover and are damaged.

Literacy Connection

Cite Textual Evidence As you read, underline the activities discussed in the text that support the idea that biodiversity has value.

Some resources in an ecosystem are used, but not consumed. These indirect values also affect the economic value. Shade trees reduce utility bills and provide wind protection. Wetlands reduce soil erosion and control flooding. Hiking, touring unique habitats, and recreational activities provide revenue. The key is using these ecosystem resources for profit without destroying them.

READING CHECK **Determine Central Ideas** What makes crops a direct value from an ecosystem?

From Farm to Market

Figure 2 Disease and poor weather conditions can cause severe financial losses for farmers.

SEP Construct Explanations Would it be wise for a farmer to grow just one type of crop? Explain.

A Valuable Tree

Figure 3 Elephants eat the fruit of the balanite, or desert date, tree. The elephants then spread the seeds in their waste as they travel.

CCC Cause and Effect Consider the interdependence between the tree and the elephant. What would happen if one of the species were to decline in number?

Investigate Explore the role of keystone species in maintaining biodiversity.

Ecological Value All species function within an ecosystem. Each species performs a certain role. All species are connected and depend on each other for survival. A **keystone species** is a species that influences the survival of many other species in an ecosystem. One example of a keystone species is the African elephant.

African elephant herds appeared to be stripping vegetation from the ecosystem, thereby harming it. Some park officials wanted to control the elephant population by thinning the herds. Instead, they let the herds range freely. When the elephants uprooted trees, that made way for grasslands and smaller animals. Shrubs grew where the trees once stood and fed the animals unable to reach taller trees. Over time, the park ecosystem, **Figure 3**, returned to an ecological balance. Changes to physical and biological factors of an ecosystem, such as the number of elephants and trees, affect all of the populations within an ecosystem.

Biodiversity sustains ecosystems by protecting land and water resources, and aiding in nutrient cycling. Trees and vegetation hold soil in place to prevent erosion and landslides. Roots break up rocks to allow water to enter the soil. Animal waste sustains soil fertility. A diverse ecosystem is stable, productive, and can easily withstand environmental changes.

READING CHECK **Evaluate** Why is the elephant considered a keystone species?

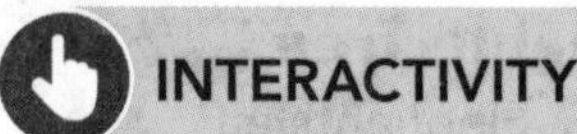

Explore the diversity of species that live in the Amazon.

Factors Affecting Biodiversity

There are numerous ecosystems on Earth. Biodiversity within these ecosystems varies from place to place. Various factors affect biodiversity, including niche diversity, genetic diversity, extinction, climate, and area.

Niche Diversity Every species in an ecosystem occupies a unique niche. The abiotic and biotic resources that a species needs to survive are provided by its niche. These resources include food, water, and habitat. The niches of different populations within an ecosystem interact with one another. Some species, like the panda in **Figure 4**, live in a narrow niche with only a few food sources. Species that have a narrow niche are more vulnerable to environmental changes. A niche can also be shared by two different species. When this happens, they compete for resources. If resources are low, one species may survive while the other must leave or die out. A healthy ecosystem reflects a balance among different populations and their unique niches.

A Narrow Niche

Figure 4 The panda's diet has no diversity. Its diet consists almost entirely of leaves, stems, and shoots from different bamboo species. Pandas can eat over 30 kg of bamboo a day. Circle the bamboo in the image.

CCC Analyze Systems What would happen to the panda population if there were a decrease in the amount of bamboo available? Explain.

....

....

....

....

....

....

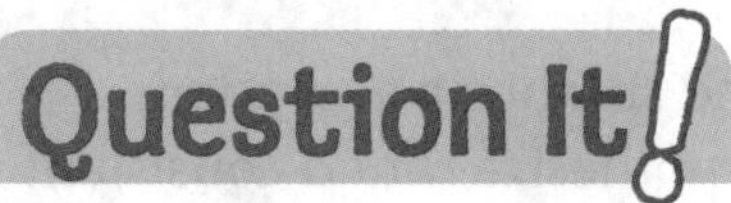

Question It!

Endangered Species

Figure 5 Cheetahs are endangered. Scientists speculate that their near-extinction status could be from their low genetic diversity, loss of natural food resources, or loss of habitat.

SEP Ask Questions A group of scientists visit your school to discuss the importance of saving the cheetah population. They need your help to design a solution to stop their declining numbers. However, you must first understand a little more about the declining cheetah populations. Each person is required to ask at least three questions of the experts to help design a solution. In the space below, write your questions. Consider constraints when developing your questions.

Genetic Diversity You may have heard the expression "gene pool." It is the number of genes available within a population. Genetic diversity, on the other hand, is the total number of inherited traits in the genetic makeup of an entire species. The greater its genetic diversity, the more likely it is that a species can adapt and survive. Species with low genetic diversity lack the ability to adapt to changing environmental conditions. The cheetahs you see in **Figure 5** have low genetic diversity, which may have contributed to their near-extinction status.

Species Extinction According to fossil evidence, over ninety percent of all organisms that have ever lived on Earth are now extinct. The disappearance of all members of a species from Earth is **extinction**. Species in danger of becoming extinct are endangered species. And species that could become endangered in the near future are threatened species. There are two ways in which species can become extinct. Background extinction occurs over a long period of time. It usually involves only one species. Environmental changes or the arrival of a competitor cause background extinctions. Mass extinction can kill many different species in a very short time. Mass extinctions are caused by rapid climate changes (such as from a meteoroid impact), continuous volcanic eruptions, or changes in the air or water.

READING CHECK **Summarize Text** Why are populations with low genetic diversity, like cheetahs, less likely to survive?

Other Factors The climate and size of an ecosystem also affect biodiversity. Scientists hypothesize that a consistent climate supports biodiversity. One of the most diverse places on Earth is the tropical rainforest. Temperatures do not fluctuate greatly and it receives a large amount of rainfall. Also, plants grow year-round, providing food for animals. An ecosystem's area, or the amount of space that an ecosystem covers, also determines its biodiversity. For example, more species are found in an ecosystem that covers 50 square kilometers, than in one that covers 10 square kilometers. An ecosystem with a larger area will generally have more biodiversity.

Math Toolbox

Room to Roam

A savanna is a grassland ecosystem with few trees. About 65 percent of Africa is covered by savannas. Lions roam where there are fewer than 25 people per square mile. As the human population in Africa increases, the amount of land where lions roam is decreasing. Use the chart and graphs to answer the questions.

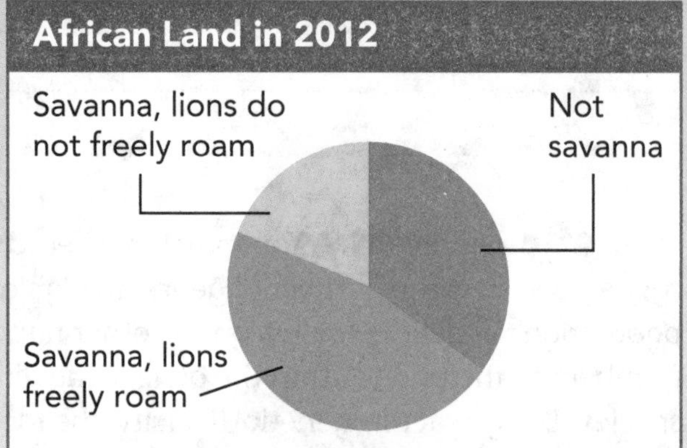

1. **Predict** Describe how the green area of the pie chart would change to show the area where lions freely roam today.

....

2. **Draw Conclusions** How has the balance in the African lion population shifted over time? What caused this shift?

....

....

....

3. **Use Ratio Reasoning** Write a ratio comparing the lion population in 1950 to 2000. Explain the relationship between human population and the lion population.

....

....

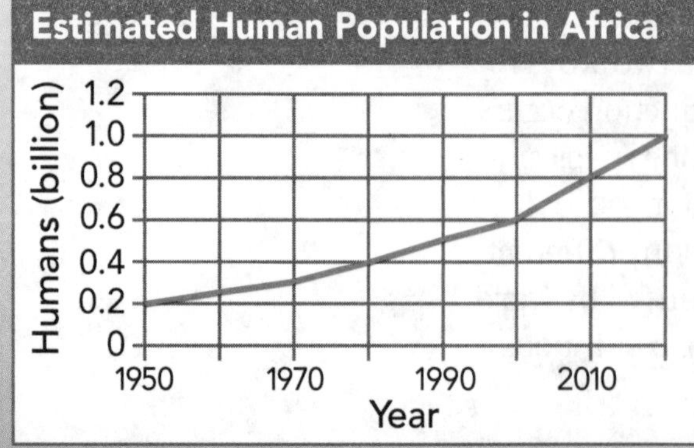

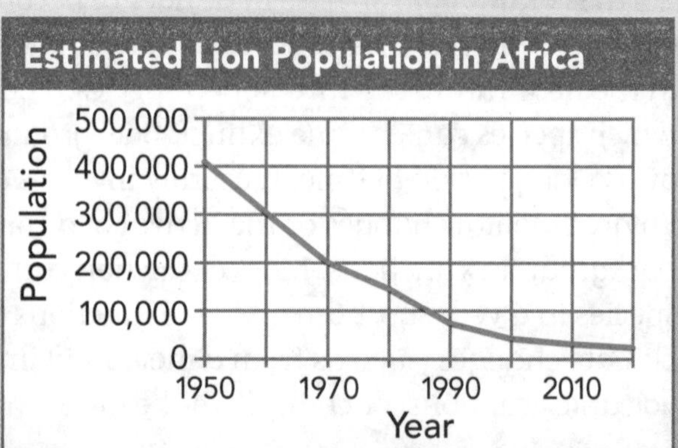

Human Impact

When an ecosystem is harmed in any way, its biodiversity is reduced. Human activities directly impact ecosystems and the organisms that live there. As you see in **Figure 6**, human activities can impact the environment.

Our Impact on Ecosystems

Figure 6 For each image, determine if the human activities are increasing or decreasing impacts on the environment. Place an "I" in the circle for an increased impact, and a "D" in the circle for a decreased impact. Then, in the space provided, provide evidence to support your determination.

Threats to Coral

Figure 7 These images show two different coral reef ecosystems. One image shows how an increase in water temperature can harm a coral reef through coral bleaching. When water gets too warm, coral can become stressed, causing the algae living in their tissue to leave. Because the coral relies on algae for food, it begins to starve. Circle the image that shows coral bleaching.

READING CHECK **Determine Conclusions** What evidence is presented to show that a warming climate can impact biodiversity?

....

....

....

....

....

....

....

Damaging Biodiversity Human activities cause most of the harm to habitats and ecosystems. The result is a loss of biodiversity. For example, removing natural resources from an ecosystem can reduce its biodiversity.

Scientists agree that increased levels of carbon dioxide gas contribute to climate change. One way humans contribute to climate change is by the removal of resources from ecosystems. For example, people remove trees for farming, houses, and timber. The use of machinery to remove and process the trees increases the amount of carbon dioxide gas in our atmosphere. In addition, the deforested plants are not taking in carbon dioxide. Changes to the climate impact all of Earth's ecosystems. It is easy to observe changes in temperature on land, but ocean water temperature also changes. **Figure 7** shows how a changing climate threatens biodiversity.

Human activities can also introduce non-native species, called **invasive species**, into a habitat. Often, invasive species out-compete native species within an ecosystem. Humans also remove species when poachers illegally kill wildlife for clothing, medicine, or body parts such as horns for ivory.

Protecting Biodiversity We can all take action to protect wildlife on Earth. For example, **Figure 8** shows students collecting data for conservation projects. Captive breeding programs help endangered species reproduce and sustain diversity. States and countries can set aside land to safeguard natural habitats. Finally, international laws and treaties protect the environment and biodiversity.

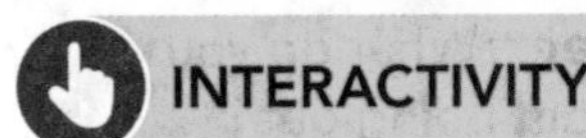

INTERACTIVITY

Examine how humans can safeguard and preserve biodiversity.

Habitat Preservation The goal of habitat preservation is to maintain the natural state of an ecosystem. Sometimes, that requires restoring its biodiversity. National parks, marine fisheries, and wildlife refuges are areas that preserve habitats. These areas are wildlife sanctuaries. Laws prevent or severely restrict any removal of resources from wildlife sanctuaries.

Citizen Scientists

Figure 8 Scientists often seek help from people like you for preservation and conservation efforts. Citizens are trained to collect data on factors such as water quality, population numbers, and behavior of species. Scientists use data to track populations and to monitor preservation efforts.

SEP Engage in Argument Do you think citizen volunteers should participate in citizen science projects? Explain.

....

....

....

....

Reflect What do you value about being out in nature? Consider the number and variety of species you see when you are outside. What would happen if some of them disappeared?

Global Cooperation Habitat preservation is critical to maintain our existing species and protect biodiversity globally. There are two treaties that are dedicated to preserving global biodiversity. The Convention on Biological Diversity focuses on conservation. The Convention on International Trade in Endangered Species of Wild Fauna and Flora ensures that the trade of plants and animals does not endanger them. These two treaties protect over 30,000 plant and animal species. We all benefit from global efforts that protect Earth's biodiversity (**Figure 9**). Protection and conservation ensure resources for future generations.

READING CHECK **Construct Explanations** Why is it important to protect marine ecosystems?

Protecting Our Oceans

Figure 9 The Sea of Cortez is a protected marine ecosystem. Global support for protecting Earth's marine ecosystems is increasing. However, gathering support is a slow process. The ocean is large and many people do not understand the importance of marine protection. Circle two organisms that could be harmed without marine protection.

LESSON 3 Check

MS-LS2-4, MS-LS2-5, MS-LS4-1

1. **SEP Construct Explanations** What is meant by the value of biodiversity?

2. **Distinguish Relationships** How is an ecosystem's biodiversity a measure of its health?

3. **CCC Cause and Effect** What consequences might occur if a particular species becomes extinct?

4. **Apply Concepts** When scientists analyze the rock record, they look for fossil evidence. How are scientists able to determine that the majority of all organisms are now extinct?

5. **SEP Engage in Argument** Support the argument that biodiversity needs to be protected. Explain.

Quest CHECK-IN

In this lesson, you learned about the value of healthy ecosystems and the importance of biodiversity. You also learned about the factors affecting biodiversity.

Synthesize Information How can road construction affect the biodiversity of an ecosystem?

HANDS-ON LAB

Design and Model a Crossing

Go online for a downloadable worksheet of this lab. Build a model of your wildlife crossing. As a class, share your ideas. Evaluate how each model functions to protect biodiversity.

Case Study

MS-LS2-2, MS-LS2-4

The Dependable Elephant

The African elephant is the largest land mammal on Earth. It can grow to weigh more than 4,500 kilograms (10,000 pounds) and spend most of its days eating. This huge creature often lives in herds of 12 to 15 individuals that are led by a dominant female. An African elephant gives birth every 3 to 4 years, producing one calf after a two-year pregnancy. A calf can weigh about 110 kilograms (250 pounds) at birth.

Elephants serve an ecological role as big as their size. As a keystone species, they directly impact the structure, composition, and biodiversity of their ecosystem—where the vast grassy plains of the African savannas and woodlands meet. Elephants affect the variety and amount of trees that make up a forest. By pulling down trees and tearing up thorny bushes, they create grassland habitats for other species. Elephant dung enriches the soil with nutrients and carries the seeds of many plant species. In fact, some of the seeds need to pass through the elephant's digestive system to germinate! Other seeds are removed from the dung and eaten by other animals. Scientists estimate that at least one-third of Africa's woodlands depend on elephants for their survival in one way or another.

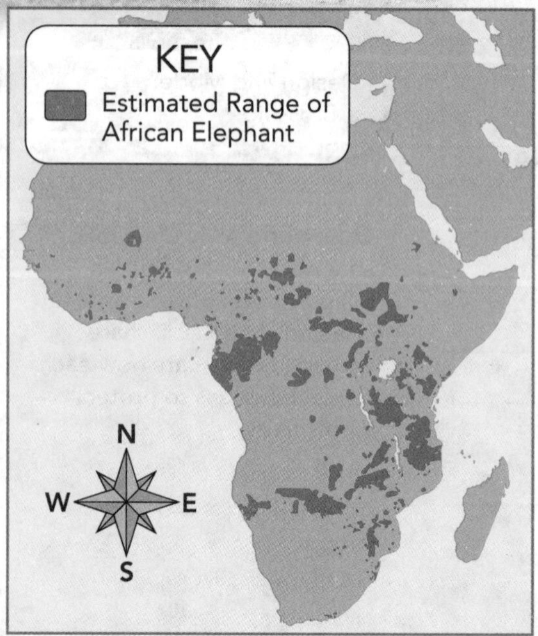

African elephants once numbered in the millions, but the numbers have been dropping. This dramatic decline is a result of poaching. Hunters kill the elephants for their ivory tusks. The valuable ivory is sold or used to make decorative items.

Saving the Elephants

Various elephant conservation groups suggest that there are scattered pockets of African elephants throughout the southern portions of the continent. While there are efforts being made to protect the elephants, there are just too few people and too much land to cover to be very effective.

The graph to the right shows the estimated African elephant population from 1995 through 2014. Use the graph to answer the questions.

African Elephant Population Trends, 1995–2014

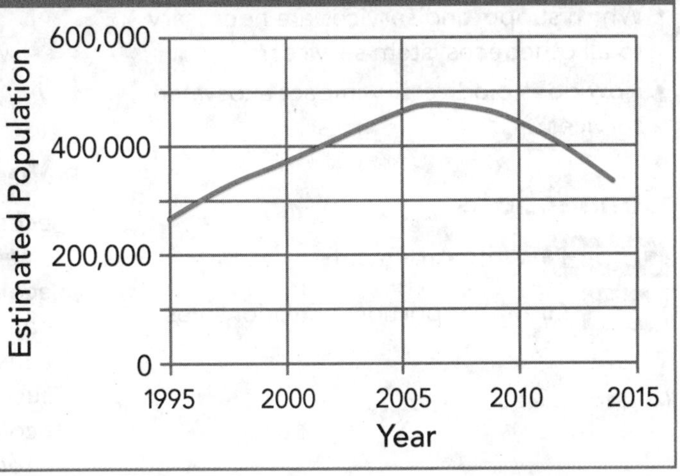

Source: US National Library of Medicine and National Institutes of Health

1. **Patterns** Describe any patterns you see in the graph.

2. **Predict** Do you think the trend shown in the graph will continue? Explain.

3. **Construct Explanations** Based on the data, how might the rest of the elephant's ecosystem be affected long term?

4. **Solve Problems** What are some ways elephants could be protected in order to preserve the biodiversity of an ecosystem?

LESSON 4

Ecosystem Services

Guiding Questions

- Why is it important to maintain healthy ecosystems?
- Which supporting services are necessary to all other ecosystem services?
- How does biodiversity impact ecosystem services?

Connections

Literacy Write Arguments

Math Graph Proportional Relationships

MS-LS2-3, MS-LS2-5

HANDS-ON LAB

uInvestigate Model how wetlands help with water purification.

Vocabulary

ecosystem services
ecology
natural resource
conservation
sustainability
ecological restoration

Academic Vocabulary

regulation

Connect It!

Circle three different organisms interacting with their environment.

Distinguish Relationships Describe how each organism interacts with the environment. How would they be affected if the environment was disrupted?

....

....

....

....

Ecosystem Services

Ecosystems meet our needs by supplying us with water, fuel, and wellness. **Ecosystem services** are the benefits humans receive from ecosystems. They are often produced without help from humans, and they are free! Ecosystem services occur because systems in an ecosystem interact with one another. Plants interact with the air, sun, soil, water, and minerals. Animals interact with plants, other animals, the air, and water. Because services are exchanged when interactions occur, biodiversity is an important factor.

In an ecosystem, all organisms, including humans, interact with one another and benefit from those interactions. **Ecology** is the study of how organisms interact with their environment. Ecology helps us understand how services emerge from those interactions. For example, the bee in **Figure 1** is pollinating the flower, but it is also getting nectar from the flower. Both interactions can result in services that humans use. Further, their exchange is an example of cycling matter and energy within an ecosystem.

Humans rely on cycling of matter and energy that occurs in diverse ecosystems. Scientists have separated ecosystem services into four categories, based on how they benefit us. The categories are: cultural, provisional, regulatory, and supporting services. Identifying and protecting each service is vital for human life.

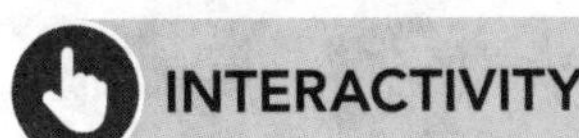

INTERACTIVITY

Explore the services provided by a healthy ecosystem.

Ecosystem Services

Figure 1 Organisms interact with and rely on one another. This bee pollinates the flower, which will turn into a blueberry. Consider some benefits you might get from this ecosystem. Some of these benefits might be obvious, while others may not be.

Cultural and Provisional Services

Figure 2 ✏ Cultural services make us feel well, while provisional services provide us with something to use. Circle any photo that shows a provisional service.

SEP Provide Evidence Which services, cultural or provisional, do humans pay the most money for? Explain.

....

....

....

....

....

....

Cultural Services Nature has a way of putting a smile on your face. When nature makes you happy, it is providing you with a cultural service. Cultural services include recreational services, such as paddling a canoe at a local lake or going on a hike, and educational services, such as exploring Earth's history in the rock layers. We use cultural services to rest and relax, or learn more about the world around us. We can even learn about history, such as the role of the Mississippi and Missouri Rivers in building our nation. **Figure 2** shows a few examples of the cultural services that give meaning to life and help our wellness.

Provisional Services *Provisional* means useful. Provisional services, also shown in **Figure 2**, are the products obtained from the natural resources in an ecosystem. Anything naturally occurring in the environment that humans use is a **natural resource**, such as drinking water, food, fuel, and raw materials. Filtered ground water and surface water are two sources we tap into for drinking water. Farming provides many of the meats, vegetables, and fruits we eat. Marine and freshwater ecosystems provide us with meat and vegetables. Fuel resources include oil, coal, and natural gas. Plants provide us with timber for buildings and plant-based medicines.

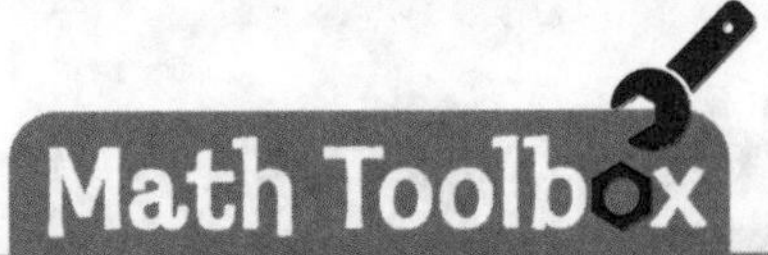

Restoring Water

The water flowing into New York Harbor is polluted due to waste and fertilizer runoff. Scientists have designed a solution that relies on natural filtration and purification. One oyster filters about 150 liters of water a day, while one mussel filters 65 liters a day.

1. **Write an Expression** Write a formula to show the amount of water filtered by 7 oysters in one day.

....

....

2. **Graph Proportional Relationships** Use your formula to calculate the amount of water 5, 10, 15, and 20 oysters can filter. Then, calculate that amount of water the same number of mussels can filter. Graph your data. Use a solid line to represent the oysters and a dashed line to represent the mussels.

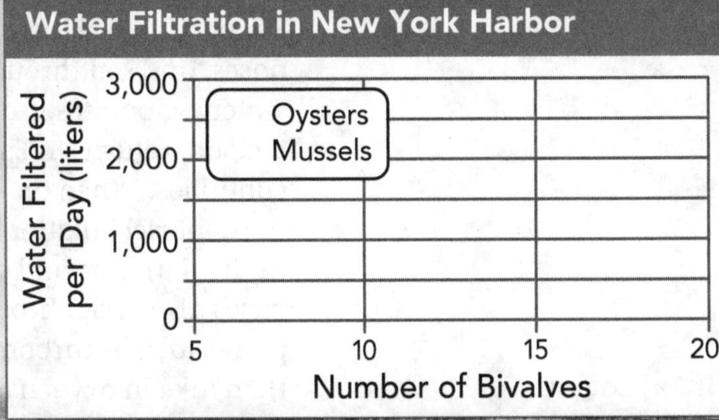

Regulatory Services

Regulatory Services Benefits humans receive from natural processes are regulatory services. An ecosystem needs to function and operate properly to support life. Many of these processes, such as decomposition, go unseen. Regulatory services allow nature to resist or fix problems that may harm the ecosystem. These processes also protect humans from some of the same problems.

Plants and animals play a major role in the regulation of an ecosystem. Plants increase air quality by removing harmful chemicals and releasing useful chemicals. They regulate our climate by absorbing a greenhouse gas—carbon dioxide. The roots of plants prevent soil erosion. Bivalves, such as mussels and oysters, filter polluted and contaminated water. We have fruits to eat because animals pollinate flowers and help disperse seeds. Some animals naturally help with pest and disease control. This natural regulation of pests is biological control.

VIRTUAL LAB

Test and evaluate competing solutions for preventing soil erosion to protect cropland.

READING CHECK **Cite Textual Evidence** How are regulatory services important for ecosystems?

....

....

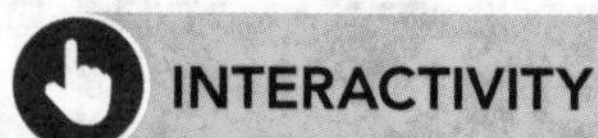

Explore the four key ecosystem services.

Supporting Services The most important ecosystem services are the ones that support all the processes in nature. While supporting services do not directly impact humans, ecosystems would cease to function without them.

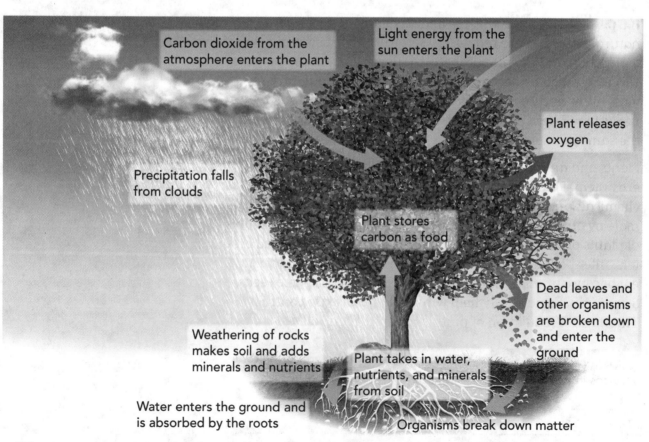

Supporting services cycle resources such as water, nutrients, gases, and soil throughout the ecosystem. In the water cycle, water evaporates, travels into the air and forms a part of a cloud, returns to Earth as precipitation, and the cycle continues. When an organism dies, it decomposes and forms nutrient-rich matter that becomes part of the soil. Plants take in the nutrients and store them in their cells. Atmospheric gases also cycle through ecosystems. During photosynthesis, plants take in carbon dioxide and release oxygen. Animals then take in oxygen and release carbon dioxide. Soil is also cycled. It is formed from weathered rock and organic matter. Rock sediment can reform into another rock with added heat and/or pressure. **Figure 3** shows how these different cycles interact with one another. The cycles ensure that matter and energy are endlessly transferred within a healthy ecosystem.

READING CHECK **Determine Central Ideas** Why are supporting services important to the ecosystem?

....

....

Interactions Between Cycles of an Ecosystem

Figure 3 Draw two arrows to show the flow of water in this ecosystem.

Explain Phenomena What would happen if any of these services were disrupted?

....

....

....

Carbon dioxide from the atmosphere enters the plant
Light energy from the sun enters the plant
Plant releases oxygen
Precipitation falls from clouds
Plant stores carbon as food
Dead leaves and other organisms are broken down and enter the ground
Weathering of rocks makes soil and adds minerals and nutrients
Plant takes in water, nutrients, and minerals from soil
Water enters the ground and is absorbed by the roots
Organisms break down matter

Biodiversity in Ecosystems

Figure 4 The survival of marine ecosystems, like this coral reef, is dependent on the diversity of organisms. Coral reefs provide every type of ecosystem service. But sometimes those services can be in conflict. People who snorkel and scuba dive can damage the corals. Boats can increase water pollution. People can also overfish the area.

Specify Design Constraints Think about ways to preserve this ecosystem. What sort of management plan could maintain the ecosystem services a coral reef provides, while protecting it from the negative impact of human activities?

Factors Impacting Ecosystem Services

Earth needs diverse and healthy ecosystems. All organisms depend on their environment to get food, water, and shelter. Diverse ecosystems provide these basic needs for life.

Biodiversity Ecosystem production increases with biodiversity. When production increases, ecosystem services increase. Coral reefs, such as the one you see in **Figure 4**, cover less than one percent of the ocean. However, over 25 percent of the marine life lives among coral reefs. Each species plays a role within the ecosystem and they benefit from one another. Small fish eat algae, so the coral do not compete for resources with algae. Predators, such as sharks, keep the number of small fish from getting too large. Some fish eat parasites growing on other fish. Organisms like crabs feed on dead organisms.

As you can see, there are many more examples of biodiversity found at coral reefs. This biodiversity helps coral reefs survive changing conditions. However, coral reefs are increasingly threatened by our demand for their resources.

Avocado Farms

Figure 5 Avocado farmers in Mexico did not know that the roots of the native trees filter water. Avocado tree roots are not able to filter the ground water.

CCC Identify Patterns How has this impacted people who rely on naturally filtered drinking water?

....

....

....

....

HANDS-ON LAB

Investigate Model how wetlands help with water purification.

Literacy Connection

Write Arguments Use the Internet to conduct research on the clearing of forests to create farmland. Research two opposing sides of the issue. Select one side of the issue to support. Using evidence, explain why you chose that side.

Human Activities When humans alter or destroy habitats, the natural cycling of the ecosystem is disrupted. The severe impact of human activities is mostly due to our ignorance and greed. Removing species from ecosystems disrupts natural cycling, which decreases ecosystem services. However, many people are working to restore and protect the natural cycling of ecosystems.

We once thought that our oceans could handle anything we dumped in them, from sewage to nuclear waste. We also assumed there would be an endless supply of goods. But by polluting our oceans, we have lost marine organisms. We have also overfished the Atlantic cod, bluefin tuna, and Chilean sea bass. Our demand has caused their populations to decline drastically.

Changing the ecosystem impacts humans because it reduces the ecosystem services we rely on. The development of cities and demand for food further harms ecosystems. When buildings replace wetlands and floodplains, flooding and loss of biodiversity often result. To grow crops, farmers strip the land of native plant species, decreasing biodiversity. In Mexico, this became a problem when avocado farmers cleared native oak and pine trees to grow avocado trees, as shown in **Figure 5**.

READING CHECK **Summarize Text** What impact do farms have on an ecosystem?

....

....

Conservation

Over the past 50 years, human activities have drastically changed Earth's ecosystems. Scientists and engineers are working to design solutions to help save Earth's ecosystems. One way is through **conservation**, or the practice of using less of a resource so that it can last longer. As concerned citizens, we can all participate in conservation to protect and restore Earth's ecosystems.

INTERACTIVITY

Investigate how biodiversity impacts ecosystem services.

Protection Healthy ecosystems need protection from the loss of resources. **Sustainability** is the ability of an ecosystem to maintain biodiversity and production indefinitely. Designating protected areas and regulating the amount of resources humans can take from an ecosystem are two main efforts to promote sustainability. The **regulation** of protected areas can be difficult to enforce without monitors.

Academic Vocabulary

Why is it important for the school to have regulations?

....

....

....

Restoration **Ecological restoration** is the practice of helping a degraded or destroyed ecosystem recover from damage. Some recovery efforts are easy, like planting native plants. Others are more difficult. For example, toxic chemical spills require bioremediation, a technique that uses microorganisms to breakdown pollutants. Restoring land to a more natural state, or land reclamation, also helps ecosystems (**Figure 6**).

READING CHECK **Determine Central Ideas** Why do scientists prefer to use bioremediation to clean up chemical spills?

....

....

Design It!

Ecological Restoration

Figure 6 Restoring an ecosystem often takes several years and several regulations.

Design Your Solution Construction of a shopping mall has caused the deterioration of a wetland area. A study conducted showed that runoff from paved areas is disrupting the existing wetland. Create a plan to present to local officials outlining criteria for restoring the remaining wetland.

....

....

....

☑ LESSON 4 Check

MS-LS2-3, MS-LS2-5

1. **Identify** What are the four categories of ecosystem services?

2. **SEP Provide Evidence** How do cultural services help humans?

3. **Distinguish Relationships** How are biodiversity and the cycling of matter related to maintaining ecosystem services?

4. **SEP Design Solutions** What are several ways that you could conserve water?

5. **Explain Phenomena** What are supporting services and why are they important to cultural, provisional, and regulatory services?

6. **Evaluate Proportion** Using your data from the math toolbox, which bivalve is more efficient at filtering water? Provide support.

7. **SEP Construct Explanations** What are some other organisms, aside from bivalves, that could be used to purify water? Explain the benefits of using this organism.

8. **SEP Design Solutions** A giant factory farm uses large open lagoons to treat waste from the buildings where hogs are stored. The problem is that the lagoons smell awful and, during rainstorms, they are at risk of spilling into surrounding river systems. Design a solution that resolves the smell and water contamination risk, and allows the farm to continue to raise hogs.

uEngineer It! Sustainable Design STEM

littleBits CHALLENGE

MS-LS2-4, MS-LS2-5

FROM BULLDOZERS To Biomes

VIDEO

Explore the different types of ecosystem services.

Do you know how to transform an old clay pit into lush biomes? You engineer it! The Eden Project in Cornwall, England shows us how.

The Challenge: To renew and transform land after humans have damaged it.

Phenomenon A clay pit in Cornwall had been mined for over a hundred years to make fine china and was shutting down. Mining provides access to resources, but can damage ecosystems by removing vegetation and topsoil. Mining can threaten biodiversity by destroying or fragmenting habitats, and increasing erosion and pollution.

Eden Project planners chose the clay pit to build a giant greenhouse to showcase biodiversity and the relationship between plants, people and resources.

The greenhouse represents two biomes: the rain forest biome and the Mediterranean biome. These biomes contain over a million plants and more than 5,000 different species. Visitors can learn how plants are adapted to different climates, how plants play a role in their daily lives, and how to use resources sustainably.

The top photo shows the clay pit that was transformed into the biome structures and lush vegetation of the Eden Project below.

DESIGN CHALLENGE

Can you build a model of a biome structure? Go to the Engineering Design Notebook to find out!

You have limited materials to work with: 30 toothpicks and 15 balls of clay

TOPIC 3 Review and Assess

1 Interactions in Ecosystems

MS-LS2-1, MS-LS2-2

1. To reduce competition, the role of an organism in its habitat is called its
   A. adaption. B. host.
   C. niche. D. parasite.

2. In which type of interaction do both species benefit?
   A. predation B. mutualism
   C. commensalism D. parasitism

3. Four different mammals all live among oak and maple trees in a forest. They don't seem to compete for the same foods or nesting places. Which of the following is a likely explanation for this lack of competition?
   A. The four species occupy different niches.
   B. Their small size is a limiting factor that reduces competition among them.
   C. There is no shortage of food.
   D. There is no shortage of space.

4. **CCC Cause and Effect** Why is it in the best interest of a parasite not to kill its host? Explain.

....

....

....

5. **SEP Construct Explanations** Describe what a predatory relationship would look like in a forest ecosystem and a wetland ecosystem. Identify any similarities and differences.

....

....

....

....

....

....

2 Dynamic and Resilient Ecosystems

MS-LS2-1, MS-LS2-2, MS-LS2-4

6. The series of predictable changes that occur in a community over time is called
   A. natural selection. B. ecology.
   C. commensalism. D. succession.

7. A disruption to an established ecosystem can lead to
   A. new organisms being prevented from moving into the area.
   B. changes in the populations of the community.
   C. more resources for all the organisms that make up the community.
   D. hurricanes or volcanic eruptions.

8. A former farmland that is now home to shrubs and small trees is undergoing
   A. pioneer succession.
   B. primary succession.
   C. secondary succession.
   D. adaptive succession.

9. After a long time, a mature community is established in an ecosystem. This community will not change unless a component of the ecosystem is ....

10. **Apply Scientific Reasoning** When a disrupted part of a wetland ecosystem is left alone so that nature can help restore it to what it once was, what are people counting on occurring? Explain.

....

....

....

....

....

....

....

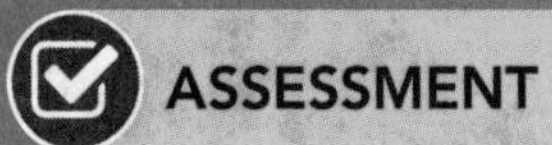

Evaluate your understanding by taking a Topic Test.

3 Biodiversity

MS-LS2-4, MS-LS2-5

11. A(n) .... is a species that influences the survival of many other species in an ecosystem.

12. A(n) .... is a non-native species that is introduced into an ecosystem and severely disrupts it by competing with native species.

13. **CCC Cause and Effect** Why are species with low genetic diversity at more risk of becoming extinct than species with high genetic diversity?

14. **Apply Concepts** Describe an example in which humans overuse an ecosystem's resources for their economic value.

4 Ecosystem Services

MS-LS2-3, MS-LS2-5

15. Going for a hike in a forest where you can breathe fresh air, observe wildlife, and relax is an example of a .... service that an ecosystem can provide.

16. The water cycle, photosynthesis, nutrient cycling, and soil formation are examples of
    A. cultural services.
    B. provisioning services.
    C. regulating services.
    D. supporting services.

17. **Analyze Properties** What are some examples of provisioning services humans get from plants?

18. **Synthesize Information** Describe an example of when land reclamation may be needed on a beach.

19. **Explain Phenomena** How can bioremediation play a role in cleaning up an oil spill?

MS-LS2-1, MS-LS2-4

Evidence-Based Assessment

Like organisms in an ecosystem, the microscopic organisms, or microbiota, living in the human mouth are affected by environmental conditions. One way the human oral environment can change is by a changing diet.

Scientists use fossil evidence to compare the oral microbiota of our ancestors with people living today. Their goal is to gain a better understanding of how the human diet has changed over time. First, they studied the diversity of oral microbiota species. They found that two cavity-causing bacteria appeared more often through time (*S. mutans* and *P. gingivalis*). Then they studied the frequency, or rate, of the two cavity-causing bacteria.

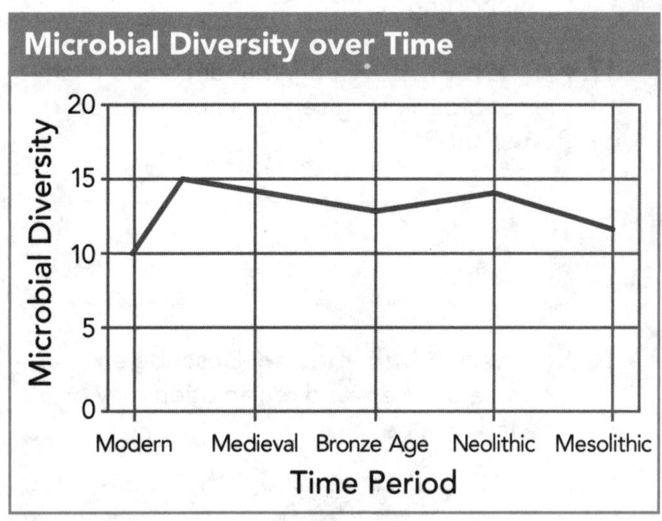

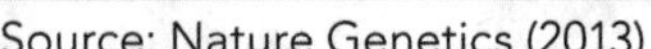
Source: Nature Genetics (2013)

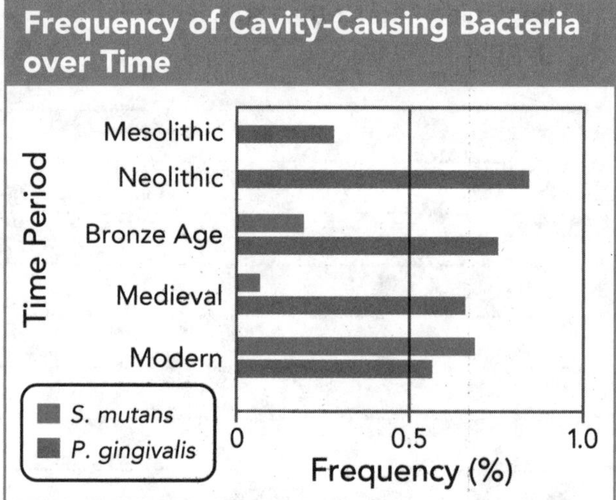

Source: Nature Genetics (2013)

The scientists also considered the changes in human diet and culture that have taken place since ancient times.

- During the Mesolithic period (7,550–5,450 BP), humans were hunter-gatherers.
- During the Neolithic period (7,400–4,000 BP), humans developed farming and adopted a carbohydrate-rich diet.
- During the Bronze Age (4,200–3,000 BP), humans manufactured bronze tools, but did not change their diet.
- During the Medieval period (1,100–400 BP), human diet was based on agricultural products.
- In modern times, humans incorporated mass-produced, commercially processed food into their diet, largely based on flour and sugar.

1. SEP Analyze Data According to the study, in which period were mouth microbiota the least diverse?
   A. Mesolithic period
   B. Neolithic period
   C. Bronze Age
   D. Medieval era
   E. Modern times

2. CCC Identify Patterns How did the frequency of each cavity-causing bacteria change over time?

3. Explain Phenomena According to the information presented in the graphs and text, what is the relationship between diet and the diversity of oral microbiota populations throughout time? Cite evidence from the graph and text.

4. SEP Communicate Information Based on the data and information presented, how did the availability of resources cause changes in the population size of cavity-causing bacteria? Explain.

Quest FINDINGS

Complete the Quest!

Phenomenon Determine the best way to clearly present your claim with data and evidence, such as graphics or a multimedia presentation.

CCC Cause and Effect If new homes or businesses are constructed when new highways are built, how would an animal crossing affect the changes to the physical and biological components of the ecosystem?

INTERACTIVITY

Reflect on Your Animal Crossing

MS-LS2-1, MS-LS2-2, MS-LS2-3, MS-LS2-4

Changes in an Ecosystem

How can you use a **model** to determine the effects of a **forest fire** on a **rabbit population**?

Background

Phenomenon Forest fires have a bad reputation! Many of these fires damage or destroy habitats and impact the populations of organisms that live there. But forest fires can also play an important role in maintaining the overall health of ecosystems. In this lab, you will develop and use a model to investigate how a forest fire might affect a population of rabbits 50 years after the fire.

Young Longleaf Pine

Tree Shadow As Seen From Above

Mature Longleaf Pine

Tree Shadow As Seen From Above

Tree Shadow As Seen From Above

(per group)

- tree-shadow circles handout
- scissors
- transparent tape

Be sure to follow all safety guidelines provided by your teacher. The Safety Appendix of your textbook provides more details about the safety icons.

Procedure

- [ ] 1. Predict what will happen to the rabbit population 50 years after the fire. Will the population be smaller, the same size, or larger? Record your prediction.
- [ ] 2. The graph paper represents the forest floor where each square is equal to 10 square meters (m^2). Calculate the total area of the forest floor. Create a data table in the space provided and enter this area in the table.
- [ ] 3. Cut out the tree shadow circles from the tree-shadow circles handout. Design a longleaf pine forest by arranging the mature pine and oak tree shadow circles on the forest floor. (Do not use the young pine tree shadows yet.) Tape the mature pine tree shadows in place, but not the oak tree shadows.
- [ ] 4. Determine the area of forest floor in sunlight. Add this data to your table.
- [ ] 5. Using a similar method, determine the square meters of shadow. Calculate the percentage of forest floor in shadow and in sunlight. Add this data to your table.
- [ ] 6. Suppose a lightning strike ignites a forest fire. Here's what would happen to some of the populations in the forest:
  - **Oak trees** are not adapted to survive fire so they burn and are destroyed; new trees will grow only if seeds are carried into the forest after the fire
  - **Longleaf pine trees** survive and continue to grow; seeds are released from pine cones and can germinate
  - **Bluestem grasses** are burned, but roots survive
- [ ] 7. Fast forward 50 years. The oak trees did not survive the forest fire, but the longleaf pines did. Use the young pine tree shadows to model the areas where young pine trees have likely grown. Repeat Steps 4 & 5 to gather evidence from your model about what the forest looks like 50 years after the fire.

HANDS-ON LAB

Demonstrate Go online for a downloadable worksheet of this lab.

Prediction

Observations

Data Table

Analyze and Interpret Data

1. **Explain** What resources are the trees and grass competing for?

2. **SEP Analyze Data** Was your prediction correct? How did resource availability 50 years after the fire impact the rabbit population? (Hint: The rabbits are herbivores that primarily feed on grasses.)

3. **SEP Cite Evidence** Use the data you have collected as evidence to support the claim you made in Question 2.

4. **SEP Engage in Argument** Longleaf pine forests are important habitats, home to several endangered species. Oak trees are invasive (non-native) species in longleaf pine forests. When there are too many oak trees, they block the sunlight that pine trees need. Construct an argument that it is sometimes necessary to set forest fires in these habitats in order to preserve these endangered species.

SEP.1, SEP.8

The Meaning of Science

Science Skills

Reflect Think about a time you misplaced something and could not find it. Write a sentence defining the problem. What science skills could you use to solve the problem? Explain how you would use at least three of the skills in the table.

Science is a way of learning about the natural world. It involves asking questions, making predictions, and collecting information to see if the answer is right or wrong.

The table lists some of the skills that scientists use. You use some of these skills every day. For example, you may observe and evaluate your lunch options before choosing what to eat.

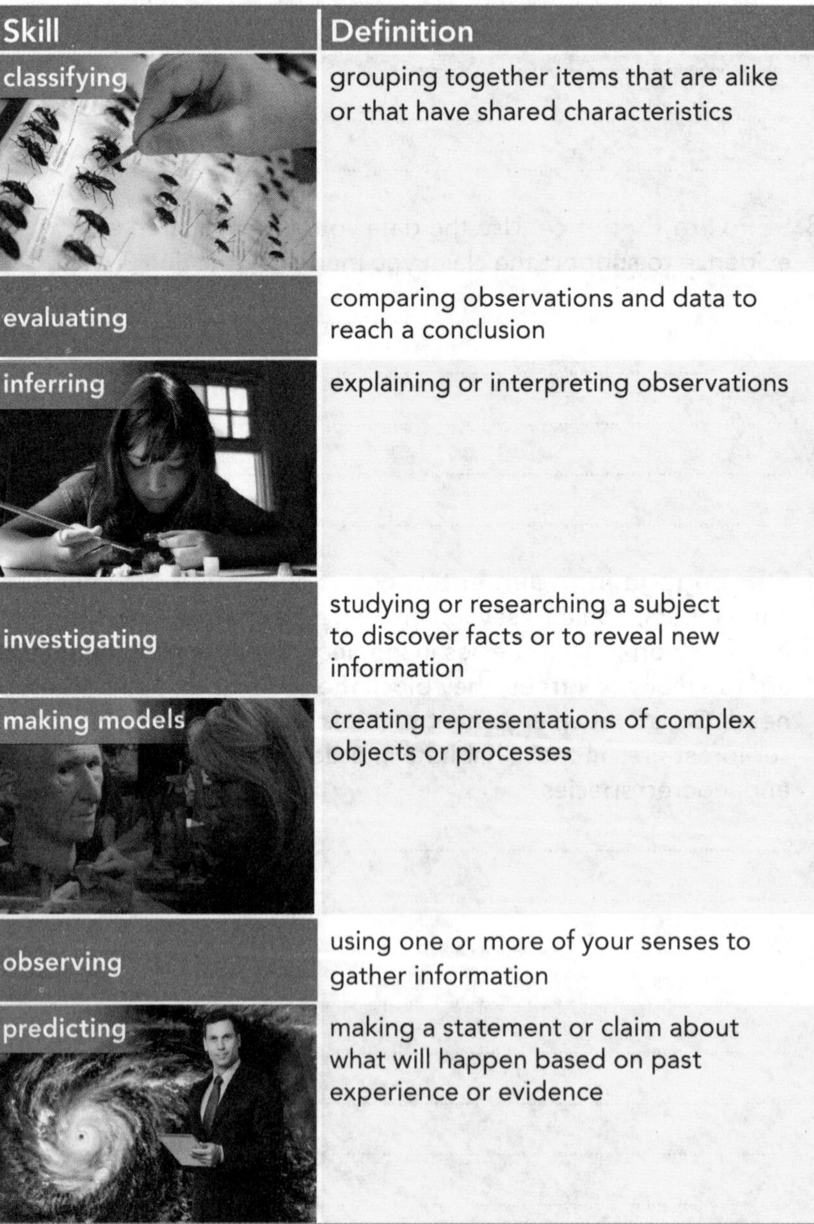

Skill	Definition
classifying	grouping together items that are alike or that have shared characteristics
evaluating	comparing observations and data to reach a conclusion
inferring	explaining or interpreting observations
investigating	studying or researching a subject to discover facts or to reveal new information
making models	creating representations of complex objects or processes
observing	using one or more of your senses to gather information
predicting	making a statement or claim about what will happen based on past experience or evidence

Scientific Attitudes

Curiosity often drives scientists to learn about the world around them. Creativity is useful for coming up with inventive ways to solve problems. Such qualities and attitudes, and the ability to keep an open mind, are essential for scientists.

When sharing results or findings, honesty and ethics are also essential. Ethics refers to rules for knowing right from wrong.

Being skeptical is also important. This means having doubts about things based on past experiences and evidence. Skepticism helps to prevent accepting data and results that may not be true.

Scientists must also avoid bias—likes or dislikes of people, ideas, or things. They must avoid experimental bias, which is a mistake that may make an experiment's preferred outcome more likely.

Make Meaning
Think about a bias the marine biologist in the photo could show that results in paying more or less attention to one kind of organism over others. Make a prediction about how that bias could affect the biologist's survey of the coral reef.

Scientific Reasoning

Scientific reasoning depends on being logical and objective. When you are objective, you use evidence and apply logic to draw conclusions. Being subjective means basing conclusions on personal feelings, biases, or opinions. Subjective reasoning can interfere with science and skew results. Objective reasoning helps scientists use observations to reach conclusions about the natural world.

Scientists use two types of objective reasoning: deductive and inductive. Deductive reasoning involves starting with a general idea or theory and applying it to a situation. For example, the theory of plate tectonics indicates that earthquakes happen mostly where tectonic plates meet. You could then draw the conclusion, or deduce, that California has many earthquakes because tectonic plates meet there.

In inductive reasoning, you make a generalization from a specific observation. When scientists collect data in an experiment and draw a conclusion based on that data, they use inductive reasoning. For example, if fertilizer causes one set of plants to grow faster than another, you might infer that the fertilizer promotes plant growth.

Write About It
Suppose it is raining when you go to sleep one night. When you wake up the next morning, you observe frozen puddles on the ground and icicles on tree branches. Use scientific reasoning to draw a conclusion about the air temperature outside. Support your conclusion using deductive or inductive reasoning.

SEP.1, SEP.2, SEP.3, SEP.4, CCC.4

Science Processes

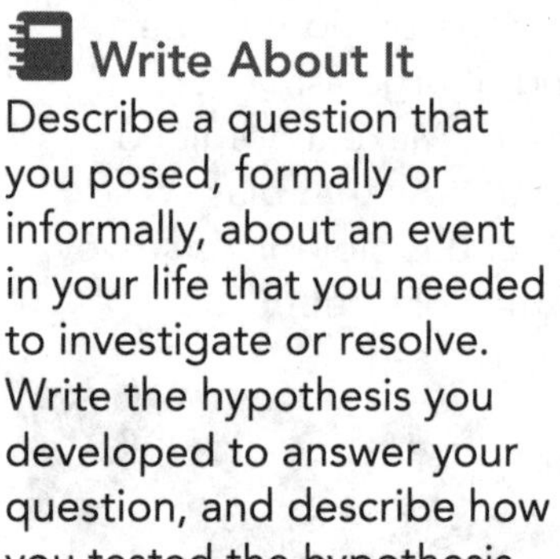

Write About It Describe a question that you posed, formally or informally, about an event in your life that you needed to investigate or resolve. Write the hypothesis you developed to answer your question, and describe how you tested the hypothesis.

Scientific Inquiry

Scientists contribute to scientific knowledge by conducting investigations and drawing conclusions. The process often begins with an observation that leads to a question, which is then followed by the development of a hypothesis. This is known as scientific inquiry.

One of the first steps in scientific inquiry is asking questions. However, it's important to make a question specific with a narrow focus so the investigation will not be too broad. A biologist may want to know all there is to know about wolves, for example. But a good, focused question for a specific inquiry might be "How many offspring does the average female wolf produce in her lifetime?"

A hypothesis is a possible answer to a scientific question. A hypothesis must be testable. For something to be testable, researchers must be able to carry out an investigation and gather evidence that will either support or disprove the hypothesis.

Scientific Models

Reflect Identify the benefits and limitations of using a plastic model of DNA, as shown here.

Models are tools that scientists use to study phenomena indirectly. A model is any representation of an object or process. Illustrations, dioramas, globes, diagrams, computer programs, and mathematical equations are all examples of scientific models. For example, a diagram of Earth's crust and mantle can help you to picture layers deep below the surface and understand events such as volcanic eruptions.

Models also allow scientists to represent objects that are either very large, such as our solar system, or very small, such as a molecule of DNA. Models can also represent processes that occur over a long period of time, such as the changes that have occurred throughout Earth's history.

Models are helpful, but they have limitations. Physical models are not made of the same materials as the objects they represent. Most models of complex objects or processes show only major parts, stages, or relationships. Many details are left out. Therefore, you may not be able to learn as much from models as you would through direct observation.

Science Experiments

An experiment or investigation must be well planned to produce valid results. In planning an experiment, you must identify the independent and dependent variables. You must also do as much as possible to remove the effects of other variables. A controlled experiment is one in which you test only one variable at a time.

For example, suppose you plan a controlled experiment to learn how the type of material affects the speed at which sound waves travel through it. The only variable that should change is the type of material. This way, if the speed of sound changes, you know that it is a result of a change in the material, not another variable such as the thickness of the material or the type of sound used.

You should also remove bias from any investigation. You may inadvertently introduce bias by selecting subjects you like and avoiding those you don't like. Scientists often conduct investigations by taking random samples to avoid ending up with biased results.

Once you plan your investigation and begin to collect data, it's important to record and organize the data. You may wish to use a graph to display and help you to interpret the data.

Write About It
List four ways you could communicate the results of a scientific study about the health of sea turtles in the Pacific Ocean.

Communicating is the sharing of ideas and results with others through writing and speaking. Communicating data and conclusions is a central part of science.

Scientists share knowledge, including new findings, theories, and techniques for collecting data. Conferences, journals, and websites help scientists to communicate with each other. Popular media, including newspapers, magazines, and social media sites, help scientists to share their knowledge with nonscientists. However, before the results of investigations are shared and published, other scientists should review the experiment for possible sources of error, such as bias and unsupported conclusions.

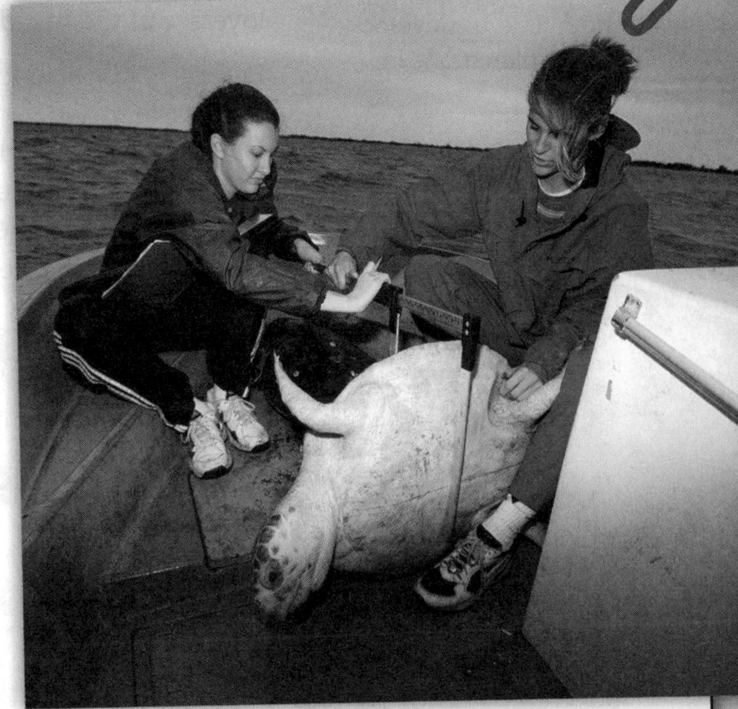

SEP.1, SEP.6, SEP.7, SEP.8

Scientific Knowledge

Scientific Explanations

Suppose you learn that adult flamingos are pink because of the food they eat. This statement is a scientific explanation—it describes how something in nature works or explains why it happens. Scientists from different fields use methods such as researching information, designing experiments, and making models to form scientific explanations. Scientific explanations often result from many years of work and multiple investigations conducted by many scientists.

Scientific Theories and Laws

A scientific law is a statement that describes what you can expect to occur every time under a particular set of conditions. A scientific law describes an observed pattern in nature, but it does not attempt to explain it. For example, the law of superposition describes what you can expect to find in terms of the ages of layers of rock. Geologists use this observed pattern to determine the relative ages of sedimentary rock layers. But the law does not explain why the pattern occurs.

By contrast, a scientific theory is a well-tested explanation for a wide range of observations or experimental results. It provides details and describes causes of observed patterns. Something is elevated to a theory only when there is a large body of evidence that supports it. However, a scientific theory can be changed or overturned when new evidence is found.

Write About It
Choose two fields of science that interest you. Describe a method used to develop scientific explanations in each field.

SEP Construct Explanations Complete the table to compare and contrast a scientific theory and a scientific law.

	Scientific Theory	Scientific Law
Definition		
Does it attempt to explain a pattern observed in nature?		

Analyzing Scientific Explanations

To analyze scientific explanations that you hear on the news or read in a book such as this one, you need scientific literacy. Scientific literacy means understanding scientific terms and principles well enough to ask questions, evaluate information, and make decisions. Scientific reasoning gives you a process to apply. This includes looking for bias and errors in the research, evaluating data, and identifying faulty reasoning. For example, by evaluating how a survey was conducted, you may find a serious flaw in the researchers' methods.

Evidence and Opinions

The basis for scientific explanations is empirical evidence. Empirical evidence includes the data and observations that have been collected through scientific processes. Satellite images, photos, and maps of mountains and volcanoes are all examples of empirical evidence that support a scientific explanation about Earth's tectonic plates. Scientists look for patterns when they analyze this evidence. For example, they might see a pattern that mountains and volcanoes often occur near tectonic plate boundaries.

To evaluate scientific information, you must first distinguish between evidence and opinion. In science, evidence includes objective observations and conclusions that have been repeated. Evidence may or may not support a scientific claim. An opinion is a subjective idea that is formed from evidence, but it cannot be confirmed by evidence.

Write About It

Suppose the conservation committee of a town wants to gauge residents' opinions about a proposal to stock the local ponds with fish every spring. The committee pays for a survey to appear on a web site that is popular with people who like to fish. The results of the survey show 78 people in favor of the proposal and two against it. Do you think the survey's results are valid? Explain.

Make Meaning

Explain what empirical evidence the photograph reveals.

SEP.3, SEP.4

Tools of Science

Measurement

Making measurements using standard units is important in all fields of science. This allows scientists to repeat and reproduce other experiments, as well as to understand the precise meaning of the results of others. Scientists use a measurement system called the International System of Units, or SI.

For each type of measurement, there is a series of units that are greater or less than each other. The unit a scientist uses depends on what is being measured. For example, a geophysicist tracking the movements of tectonic plates may use centimeters, as plates tend to move small amounts each year. Meanwhile, a marine biologist might measure the movement of migrating bluefin tuna on the scale of kilometers.

Units for length, mass, volume, and density are based on powers of ten—a meter is equal to 100 centimeters or 1000 millimeters. Units of time do not follow that pattern. There are 60 seconds in a minute, 60 minutes in an hour, and 24 hours in a day. These units are based on patterns that humans perceived in nature. Units of temperature are based on scales that are set according to observations of nature. For example, 0°C is the temperature at which pure water freezes, and 100°C is the temperature at which it boils.

Write About It
Suppose you are planning an investigation in which you must measure the dimensions of several small mineral samples that fit in your hand. Which metric unit or units will you most likely use? Explain your answer.

Measurement	Metric units
Length or distance	meter (m), kilometer (km), centimeter (cm), millimeter (mm) 1 km = 1,000 m 1 cm = 10 mm 1 m = 100 cm
Mass	kilogram (kg), gram (g), milligram (mg) 1 kg = 1,000 g 1 g = 1,000 mg
Volume	cubic meter (m^3), cubic centimeter (cm^3) 1 m^3 = 1,000,000 cm^3
Density	kilogram per cubic meter (kg/m^3), gram per cubic centimeter (g/cm^3) 1,000 kg/m^3 = 1 g/cm^3
Temperature	degrees Celsius (°C), kelvin (K) 1°C = 273 K
Time	hour (h), minute (m), second (s)

Math Skills

Using numbers to collect and interpret data involves math skills that are essential in science. For example, you use math skills when you estimate the number of birds in an entire forest after counting the actual number of birds in ten trees.

Scientists evaluate measurements and estimates for their precision and accuracy. In science, an accurate measurement is very close to the actual value. Precise measurements are very close, or nearly equal, to each other. Reliable measurements are both accurate and precise. An imprecise value may be a sign of an error in data collection. This kind of anomalous data may be excluded to avoid skewing the data and harming the investigation.

Other math skills include performing specific calculations, such as finding the mean, or average, value in a data set. The mean can be calculated by adding up all of the values in the data set and then dividing that sum by the number of values.

Hour	Number of Ducks Observed at a Pond
1	12
2	10
3	2
4	14
5	13
6	10
7	11

SEP Use Mathematics The data table shows how many ducks were seen at a pond every hour over the course of seven hours. Is there a data point that seems anomalous? If so, cross out that data point. Then, calculate the mean number of ducks on the pond. Round the mean to the nearest whole number.

....

Graphs

Graphs help scientists to interpret data by helping them to find trends or patterns in the data. A line graph displays data that show how one variable (the dependent or outcome variable) changes in response to another (the independent or test variable). The slope and shape of a graph line can reveal patterns and help scientists to make predictions. For example, line graphs can help you to spot patterns of change over time.

Scientists use bar graphs to compare data across categories or subjects that may not affect each other. The heights of the bars make it easy to compare those quantities. A circle graph, also known as a pie chart, shows the proportions of different parts of a whole.

Write About It
You and a friend record the distance you travel every 15 minutes on a one-hour bike trip. Your friend wants to display the data as a circle graph. Explain whether or not this is the best type of graph to display your data. If not, suggest another graph to use.

SEP.1, SEP.2, SEP.3, SEP.6

The Engineering Design Process

Engineers are builders and problem solvers. Chemical engineers experiment with new fuels made from algae. Civil engineers design roadways and bridges. Bioengineers develop medical devices and prosthetics. The common trait among engineers is an ability to identify problems and design solutions to solve them. Engineers use a creative process that relies on scientific methods to help guide them from a concept or idea all the way to the final product.

Define the Problem

To identify or define a problem, different questions need to be asked: *What are the effects of the problem? What are the likely causes? What other factors could be involved?* Sometimes the obvious, immediate cause of a problem may be the result of another problem that may not be immediately apparent. For example, climate change results in different weather patterns, which in turn can affect organisms that live in certain habitats. So engineers must be aware of all the possible effects of potential solutions. Engineers must also take into account how well different solutions deal with the different causes of the problem.

Reflect Write about a problem that you encountered in your life that had both immediate, obvious causes as well as less-obvious and less-immediate ones.

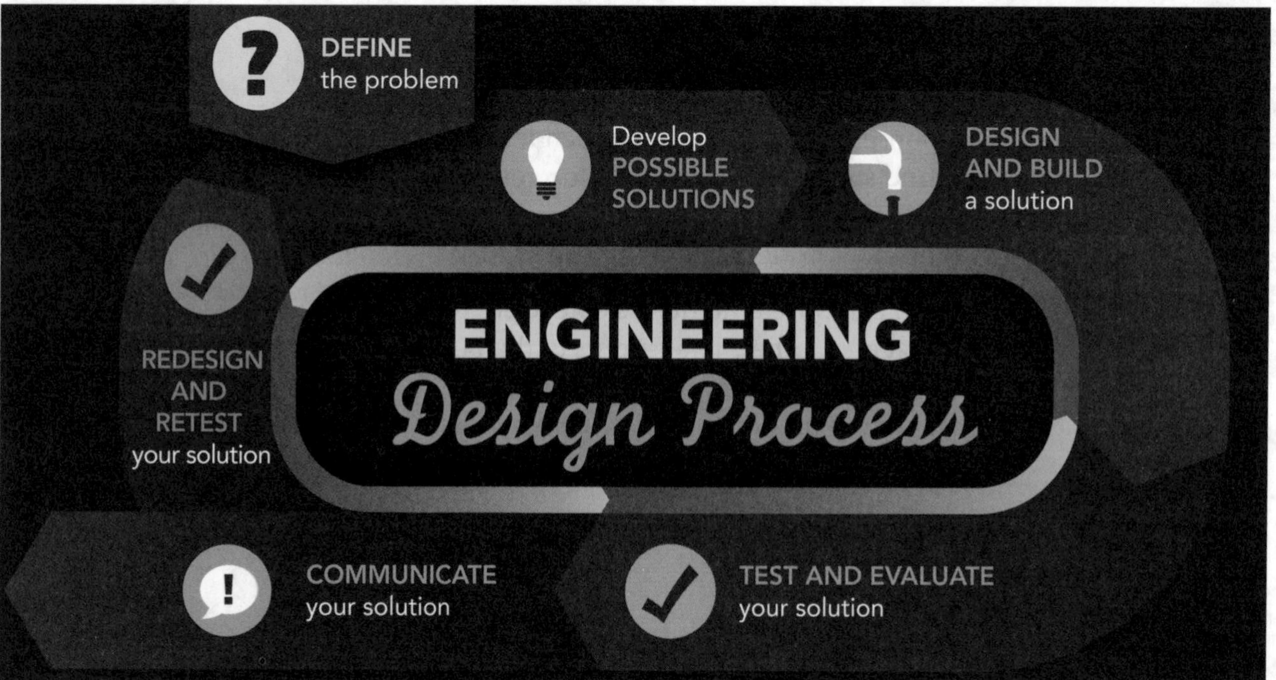

As engineers consider problems and design solutions, they must identify and categorize the criteria and constraints of the project.

Criteria are the factors that must be met or accomplished by the solution. For example, a gardener who wants to protect outdoor plants from deer and rabbits may say that the criteria for the solution are "plants are no longer eaten" and "plant growth is not inhibited in any way." The gardener then knows the plants cannot simply be sealed off from the environment, because the plants will not receive sunlight and water.

The same gardener will likely have constraints on his solution, such as budget for materials and time that is available for working on the project. By setting constraints, a solution can be designed that will be successful without introducing a new set of problems. No one wants to spend $500 on materials to protect $100 worth of tomatoes and cucumbers.

Develop Possible Solutions

After the problem has been identified, and the criteria and constraints identified, an engineer will consider possible solutions. This often involves working in teams with other engineers and designers to brainstorm ideas and research materials that can be used in the design.

It's important for engineers to think creatively and explore all potential solutions. If you wanted to design a bicycle that was safer and easier to ride than a traditional bicycle, then you would want more than just one or two solutions. Having multiple ideas to choose from increases the likelihood that you will develop a solution that meets the criteria and constraints. In addition, different ideas that result from brainstorming can often lead to new and better solutions to an existing problem.

Make Meaning
Using the example of a garden that is vulnerable to wild animals such as deer, make a list of likely constraints on an engineering solution to the problem you identified before. Determine if there are common traits among the constraints, and identify categories for them.

Design a Solution

Engineers then develop the idea that they feel best solves the problem. Once a solution has been chosen, engineers and designers get to work building a model or prototype of the solution. A model may involve sketching on paper or using computer software to construct a model of the solution. A prototype is a working model of the solution.

Building a model or prototype helps an engineer determine whether a solution meets the criteria and stays within the constraints. During this stage of the process, engineers must often deal with new problems and make any necessary adjustments to the model or prototype.

Test and Evaluate a Solution

Make Meaning Think about an aluminum beverage can. What would happen if the price or availability of aluminum changed so much that cans needed to be made of a new material? What would the criteria and constraints be on the development of a new can?

Whether testing a model or a prototype, engineers use scientific processes to evaluate their solutions. Multiple experiments, tests, or trials are conducted, data are evaluated, and results and analyses are communicated. New criteria or constraints may emerge as a result of testing. In most cases, a solution will require some refinement or revision, even if it has been through successful testing. Refining a solution is necessary if there are new constraints, such as less money or available materials. Additional testing may be done to ensure that a solution satisfies local, state, or federal laws or standards.

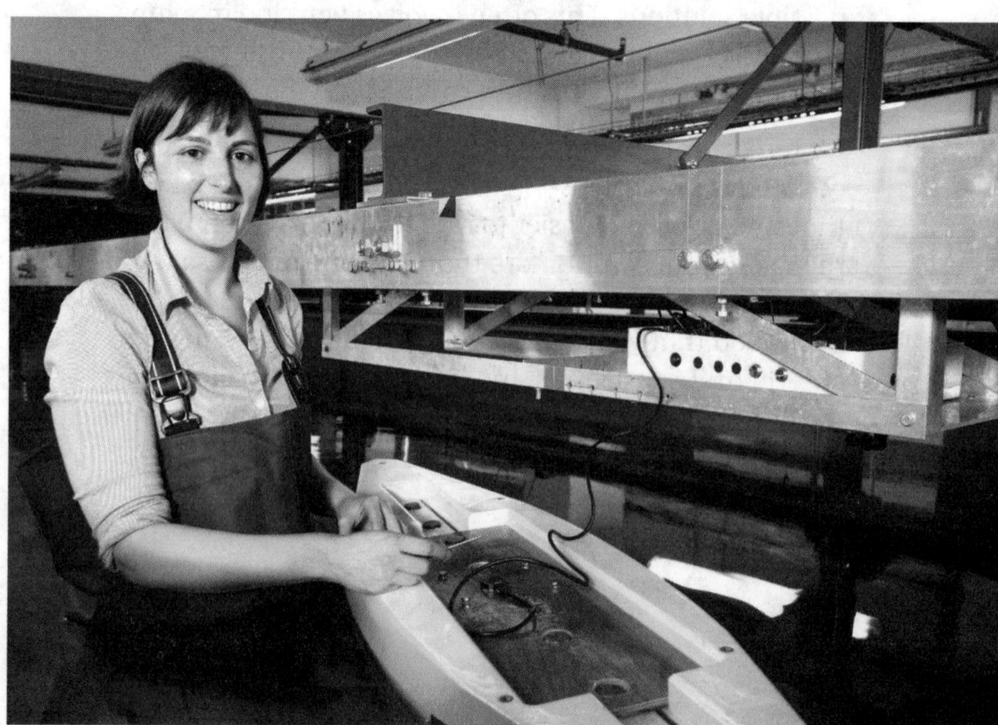

A naval architect sets up a model to test how the the hull's design responds to waves.

Communicate the Solution

Engineers need to communicate the final design to the people who will manufacture the product. This may include sketches, detailed drawings, computer simulations, and written text. Engineers often provide evidence that was collected during the testing stage. This evidence may include graphs and data tables that support the decisions made for the final design.

If there is feedback about the solution, then the engineers and designers must further refine the solution. This might involve making minor adjustments to the design, or it might mean bigger modifications to the design based on new criteria or constraints. Any changes in the design will require additional testing to make sure that the changes work as intended.

Redesign and Retest the Solution

At different steps in the engineering and design process, a solution usually must be revised and retested. Many designs fail to work perfectly, even after models and prototypes are built, tested, and evaluated. Engineers must be ready to analyze new results and deal with any new problems that arise. Troubleshooting, or fixing design problems, allows engineers to adjust the design to improve on how well the solution meets the need.

SEP Communicate Information Suppose you are an engineer at an aerospace company. Your team is designing a rover to be used on a future NASA space mission. A family member doesn't understand why so much of your team's time is taken up with testing and retesting the rover design. What are three things you would tell your relative to explain why testing and retesting are so important to the engineering and design process?

....

....

....

....

....

....

....

....

....

APPENDIX A

Safety Symbols

These symbols warn of possible dangers in the laboratory and remind you to work carefully.

Safety Goggles Wear safety goggles to protect your eyes in any activity involving chemicals, flames or heating, or glassware.

Lab Apron Wear a laboratory apron to protect your skin and clothing from damage.

Breakage Handle breakable materials, such as glassware, with care. Do not touch broken glassware.

Heat-Resistant Gloves Use an oven mitt or other hand protection when handling hot materials, such as hot plates or hot glassware.

Plastic Gloves Wear disposable plastic gloves when working with harmful chemicals and organisms. Keep your hands away from your face, and dispose of the gloves according to your teacher's instructions.

Heating Use a clamp or tongs to pick up hot glassware. Do not touch hot objects with your bare hands.

Flames Before you work with flames, tie back loose hair and clothing. Follow your teacher's instructions about lighting and extinguishing flames.

No Flames When using flammable materials, make sure there are no flames, sparks, or other exposed heat sources present.

Corrosive Chemical Avoid getting acid or other corrosive chemicals on your skin or clothing or in your eyes. Do not inhale the vapors. Wash your hands after the activity.

Poison Do not let any poisonous chemical come into contact with your skin, and do not inhale its vapors. Wash your hands when you are finished with the activity.

Fumes Work in a well-ventilated area when harmful vapors may be involved. Avoid inhaling vapors directly. Test an odor only when directed to do so by your teacher, and use a wafting motion to direct the vapor toward your nose.

Sharp Object Scissors, scalpels, knives, needles, pins, and tacks can cut your skin. Always direct a sharp edge or point away from yourself and others.

Animal Safety Treat live or preserved animals or animal parts with care to avoid harming the animals or yourself. Wash your hands when you are finished with the activity.

Plant Safety Handle plants only as directed by your teacher. If you are allergic to certain plants, tell your teacher; do not do an activity involving those plants. Avoid touching harmful plants such as poison ivy. Wash your hands when you are finished with the activity.

Electric Shock To avoid electric shock, never use electrical equipment around water, when the equipment is wet, or when your hands are wet. Be sure cords are untangled and cannot trip anyone. Unplug equipment not in use.

Physical Safety When an experiment involves physical activity, avoid injuring yourself or others. Alert your teacher if there is any reason you should not participate.

Disposal Dispose of chemicals and other laboratory materials safely. Follow the instructions from your teacher.

Hand Washing Wash your hands thoroughly when finished with an activity. Use soap and warm water. Rinse well.

General Safety Awareness When this symbol appears, follow the instructions provided. When you are asked to develop your own procedure in a lab, have your teacher approve your plan.

APPENDIX B

Using a Laboratory Balance

The laboratory balance is an important tool in scientific investigations. Different kinds of balances are used in the laboratory to determine the masses and weights of objects. You can use a triple-beam balance to determine the masses of materials that you study or experiment with in the laboratory. An electronic balance, unlike a triple-beam balance, is used to measure the weights of materials.

The triple-beam balance that you may use in your science class is probably similar to the balance depicted in this Appendix. To use the balance properly, you should learn the name, location, and function of each part of the balance.

Triple-Beam Balance

The triple-beam balance is a single-pan balance with three beams calibrated in grams. The back, or 100-gram, beam is divided into ten units of 10 grams each. The middle, or 500-gram, beam is divided into five units of 100 grams each. The front, or 10-gram, beam is divided into ten units of 1 gram each. Each gram on the front beam is further divided into units of 0.1 gram.

Apply Concepts What is the greatest mass you could find with the triple-beam balance in the picture?

....

Calculate What is the mass of the apple in the picture?

....

The following procedure can be used to find the mass of an object with a triple-beam balance:

1. Place the object on the pan.
2. Move the rider on the middle beam notch by notch until the horizontal pointer on the right drops below zero. Move the rider back one notch.
3. Move the rider on the back beam notch by notch until the pointer again drops below zero. Move the rider back one notch.
4. Slowly slide the rider along the front beam until the pointer stops at the zero point.
5. The mass of the object is equal to the sum of the readings on the three beams.

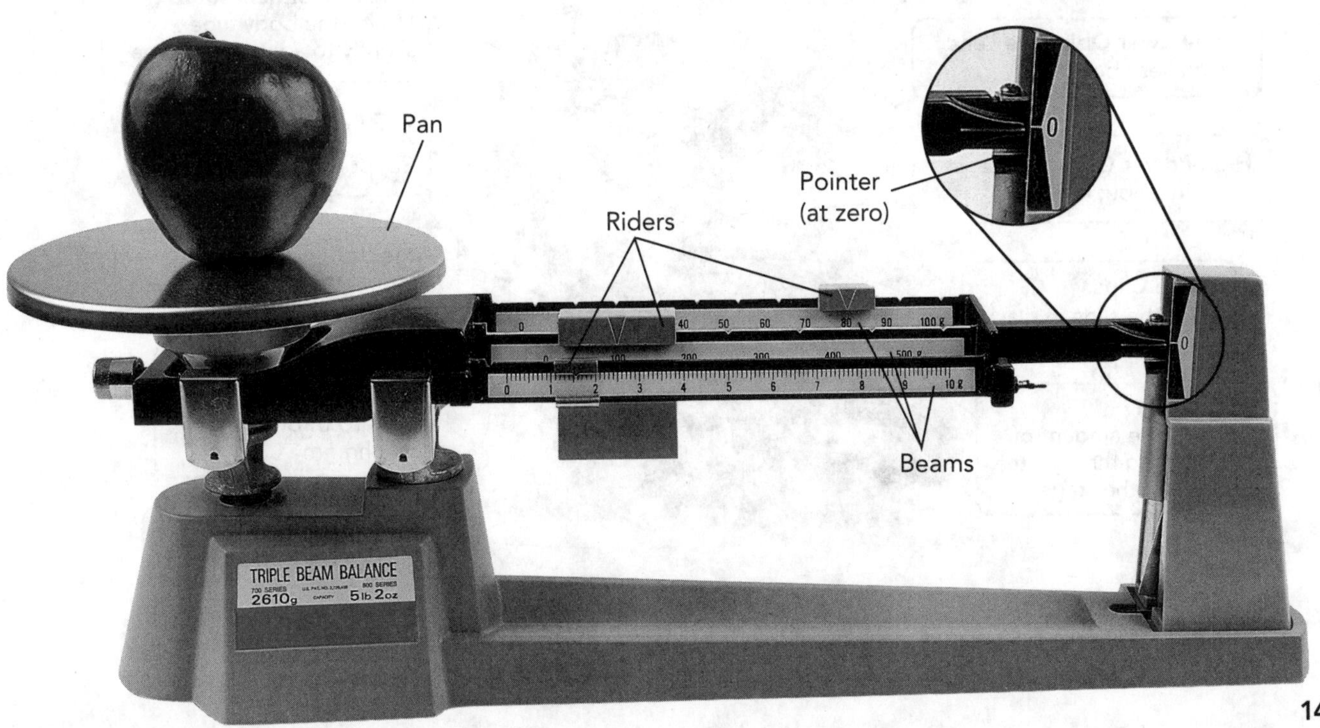

Using a Microscope

The microscope is an essential tool in the study of life science. It allows you to see things that are too small to be seen with the unaided eye.

You will probably use a compound microscope like the one you see here. The compound microscope has more than one lens that magnifies the object you view.

Typically, a compound microscope has one lens in the eyepiece (the part you look through). The eyepiece lens usually magnifies 10×. Any object you view through this lens will appear 10 times larger than it is.

A compound microscope may contain two or three other lenses called objective lenses. They are called the low-power and high-power objective lenses. The low-power objective lens usually magnifies 10×. The high-power objective lenses usually magnify 40× and 100×.

To calculate the total magnification with which you are viewing an object, multiply the magnification of the eyepiece lens by the magnification of the objective lens you are using. For example, the eyepiece's magnification of 10× multiplied by the low-power objective's magnification of 10× equals a total magnification of 100×.

Use the photo of the compound microscope to become familiar with the parts of the microscope and their functions.

The Parts of a Microscope

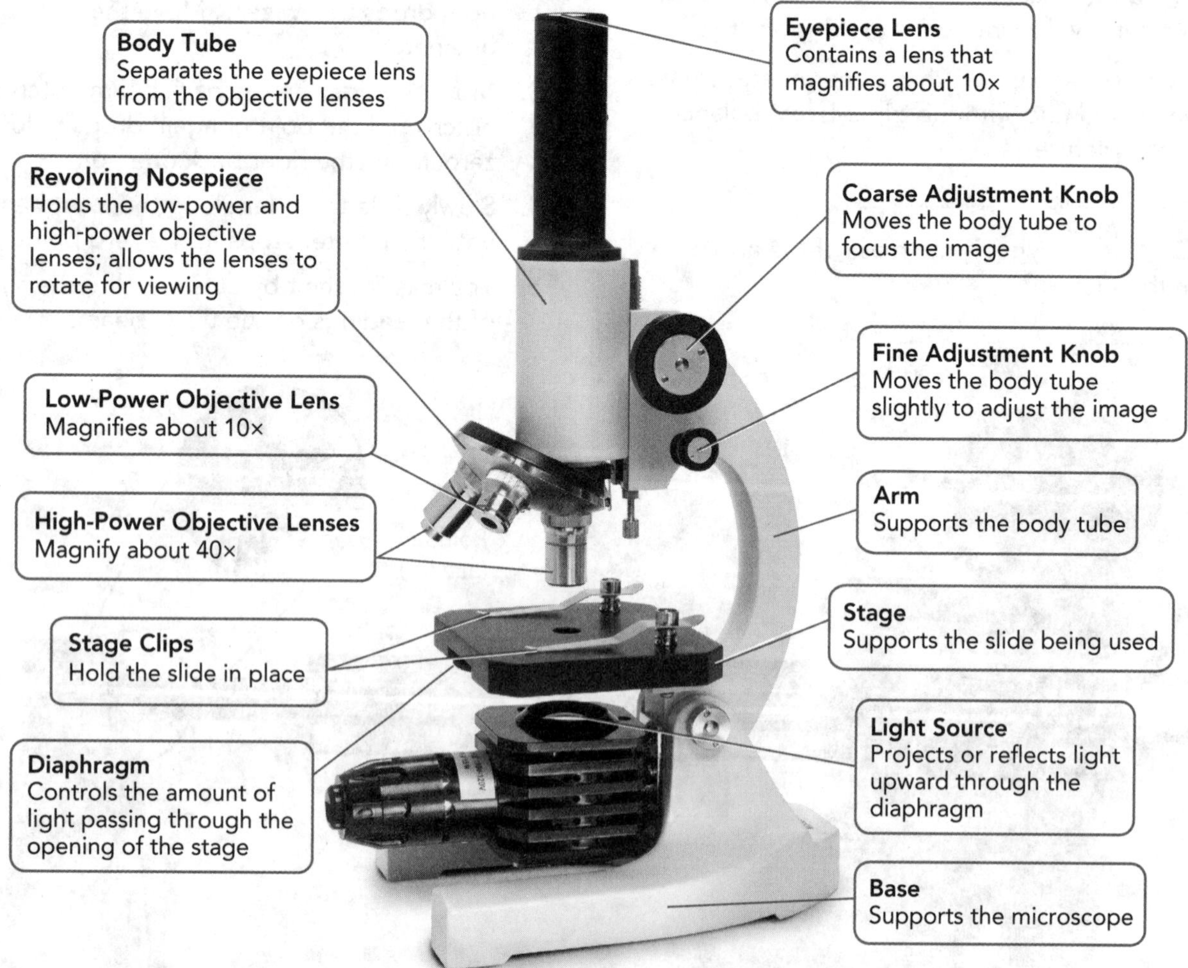
Body Tube
Separates the eyepiece lens from the objective lenses
Eyepiece Lens
Contains a lens that magnifies about 10×
Revolving Nosepiece
Holds the low-power and high-power objective lenses; allows the lenses to rotate for viewing
Coarse Adjustment Knob
Moves the body tube to focus the image
Fine Adjustment Knob
Moves the body tube slightly to adjust the image
Low-Power Objective Lens
Magnifies about 10×
Arm
Supports the body tube
High-Power Objective Lenses
Magnify about 40×
Stage
Supports the slide being used
Stage Clips
Hold the slide in place
Light Source
Projects or reflects light upward through the diaphragm
Diaphragm
Controls the amount of light passing through the opening of the stage
Base
Supports the microscope

Using the Microscope

Use the following procedures when you are working with a microscope.

1. To carry the microscope, grasp the microscope's arm with one hand. Place your other hand under the base.
2. Place the microscope on a table with the arm toward you.
3. Turn the coarse adjustment knob to raise the body tube.
4. Revolve the nosepiece until the low-power objective lens clicks into place.
5. Adjust the diaphragm. While looking through the eyepiece, adjust the mirror until you see a bright white circle of light. **CAUTION:** Never use direct sunlight as a light source.
6. Place a slide on the stage. Center the specimen over the opening on the stage. Use the stage clips to hold the slide in place. **CAUTION:** Glass slides are fragile.
7. Look at the stage from the side. Carefully turn the coarse adjustment knob to lower the body tube until the low-power objective almost touches the slide.
8. Looking through the eyepiece, very slowly turn the coarse adjustment knob until the specimen comes into focus.
9. To switch to the high-power objective lens, look at the microscope from the side. Carefully revolve the nosepiece until the high-power objective lens clicks into place. Make sure the lens does not hit the slide.
10. Looking through the eyepiece, turn the fine adjustment knob until the specimen comes into focus.

Making a Wet-Mount Slide

Use the following procedures to make a wet-mount slide of a specimen.

1. Obtain a clean microscope slide and a coverslip. **CAUTION:** Glass slides and coverslips are fragile.
2. Place the specimen on the center of the slide. The specimen must be thin enough for light to pass through it.
3. Using a plastic dropper, place a drop of water on the specimen.
4. Gently place one edge of the coverslip against the slide so that it touches the edge of the water drop at a 45° angle. Slowly lower the coverslip over the specimen. If you see air bubbles trapped beneath the coverslip, tap the coverslip gently with the eraser end of a pencil.
5. Remove any excess water at the edge of the coverslip with a paper towel.

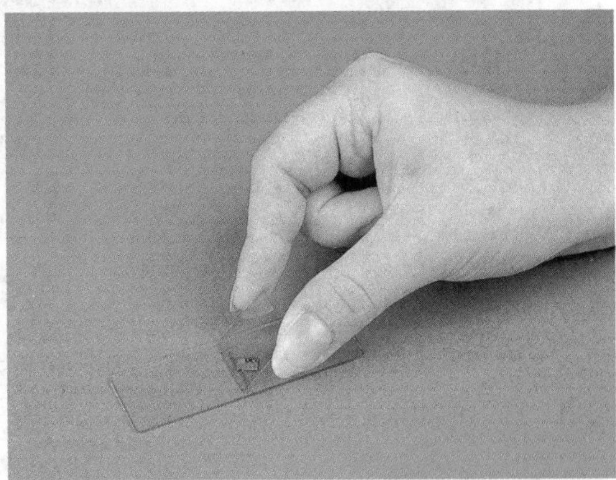

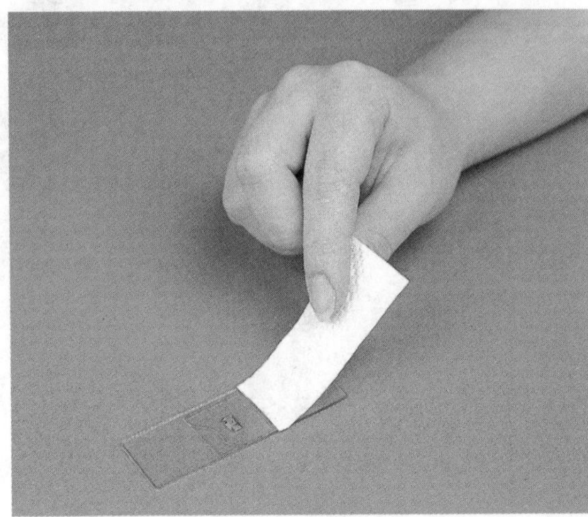

Periodic Table of Elements

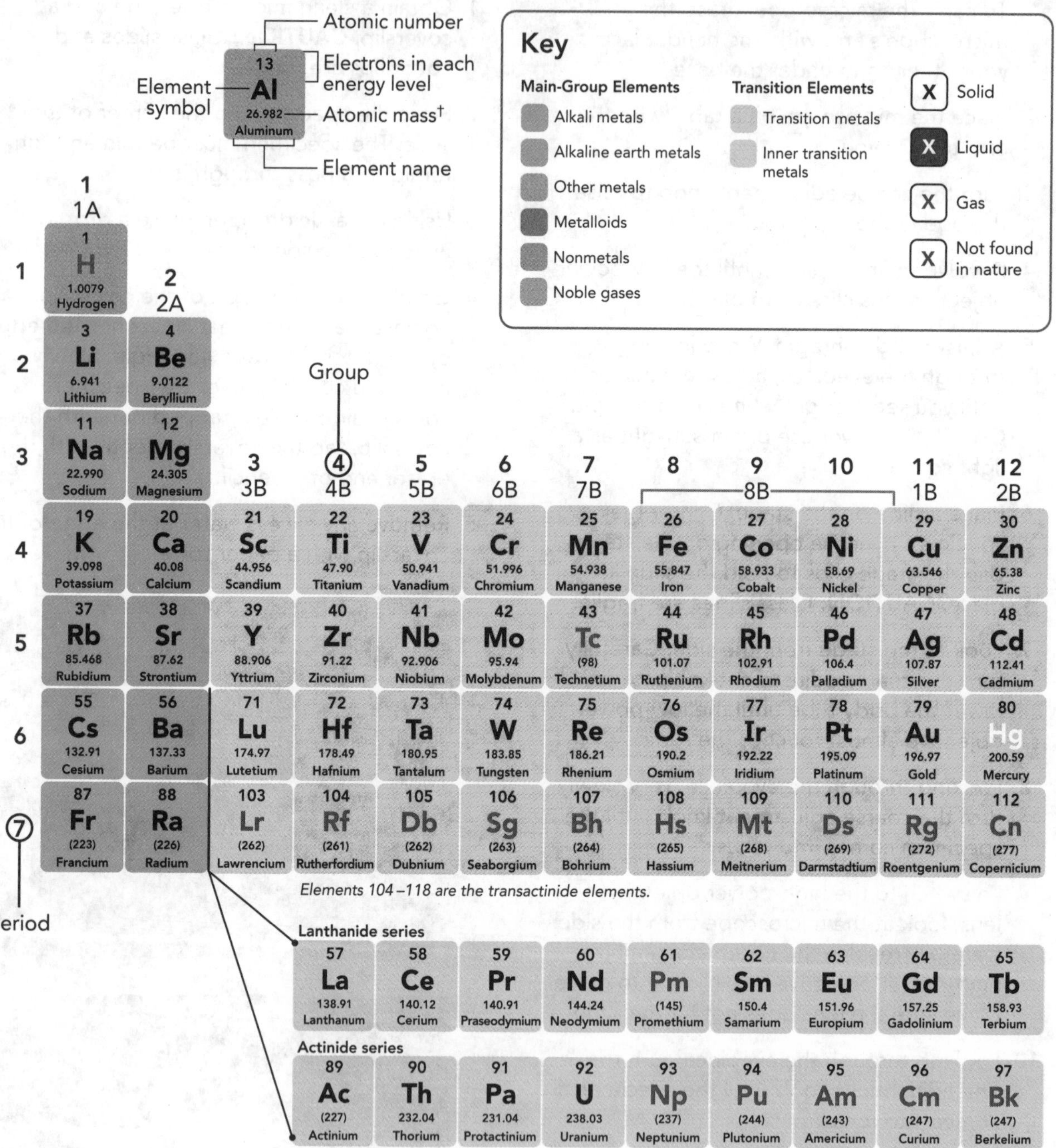

†The atomic masses in parentheses are the mass numbers of the longest-lived isotope of elements for which a standard atomic mass cannot be defined.

13 3A	14 4A	15 5A	16 6A	17 7A	18 8A
					2 **He** 4.0026 Helium
5 **B** 10.81 Boron	6 **C** 12.011 Carbon	7 **N** 14.007 Nitrogen	8 **O** 15.999 Oxygen	9 **F** 18.998 Fluorine	10 **Ne** 20.179 Neon
13 **Al** 26.982 Aluminum	14 **Si** 28.086 Silicon	15 **P** 30.974 Phosphorus	16 **S** 32.06 Sulfur	17 **Cl** 35.453 Chlorine	18 **Ar** 39.948 Argon
31 **Ga** 69.72 Gallium	32 **Ge** 72.59 Germanium	33 **As** 74.922 Arsenic	34 **Se** 78.96 Selenium	35 **Br** 79.904 Bromine	36 **Kr** 83.80 Krypton
49 **In** 114.82 Indium	50 **Sn** 118.69 Tin	51 **Sb** 121.75 Antimony	52 **Te** 127.60 Tellurium	53 **I** 126.90 Iodine	54 **Xe** 131.30 Xenon
81 **Tl** 204.37 Thallium	82 **Pb** 207.2 Lead	83 **Bi** 208.98 Bismuth	84 **Po** (209) Polonium	85 **At** (210) Astatine	86 **Rn** (222) Radon
113 **Nh** (284) Nihonium	114 **Fl** (289) Flerovium	115 **Mc** (288) Moscovium	116 **Lv** (292) Livermorium	117 **Ts** (294) Tennessine	118 **Og** (294) Oganesson

66 **Dy** 162.50 Dysprosium	67 **Ho** 164.93 Holmium	68 **Er** 167.26 Erbium	69 **Tm** 168.93 Thulium	70 **Yb** 173.04 Ytterbium
98 **Cf** (251) Californium	99 **Es** (252) Einsteinium	100 **Fm** (257) Fermium	101 **Md** (258) Mendelevium	102 **No** (259) Nobelium

GLOSSARY

A

abiotic factor A nonliving part of an organism's habitat. (38)

autotroph An organism that is able to capture energy from sunlight or chemicals and use it to produce its own food. (7)

B

biodiversity The number and variety of different species in an area. (97)

biotic factor A living or once living part of an organism's habitat. (38)

C

cellular respiration The process in which oxygen and glucose undergo a complex series of chemical reactions inside cells, releasing energy. (17)

chlorophyll A green photosynthetic pigment found in the chloroplasts of plants, algae, and some bacteria. (8)

commensalism A type of symbiosis between two species in which one species benefits and the other species is neither helped nor harmed. (84)

community All the different populations that live together in a certain area. (39)

competition The struggle between organisms to survive as they attempt to use the same limited resources in the same place at the same time. (81)

condensation The change in state from a gas to a liquid. (59)

conservation The practice of using less of a resource so that it can last longer. (117)

consumer An organism that obtains energy by feeding on other organisms. (48)

D

decomposer An organism that gets energy by breaking down biotic wastes and dead organisms and returns raw materials to the soil and water. (49)

E

ecological restoration The practice of helping a degraded or destroyed ecosystem recover from damage. (117)

ecology The study of how organisms interact with each other and their environment. (111)

ecosystem The community of organisms that live in a particular area, along with their nonliving environment. (39)

ecosystem services The benefits that humans derive from ecosystems. (111)

energy pyramid A diagram that shows the amount of energy that moves from one feeding level to another in a food web. (52)

evaporation The process by which molecules at the surface of a liquid absorb enough energy to change to a gas. (58)

extinction The disappearance of all members of a species from Earth. (101)

F

fermentation The process by which cells release energy by breaking down food molecules without using oxygen. (21)

food chain A series of events in an ecosystem in which organisms transfer energy by eating and by being eaten. (50)

food web The pattern of overlapping feeding relationships or food chains among the various organisms in an ecosystem. (50)

H

habitat An environment that provides the things a specific organism needs to live, grow, and reproduce. (37)

heterotroph An organism that cannot make its own food and gets food by consuming other living things. (7)

I

invasive species Species that are not native to a habitat and can out-compete native species in an ecosystem. (104)

K

keystone species A species that influences the survival of many other species in an ecosystem. (99)

L

law of conservation of energy The rule that energy cannot be created or destroyed. (57)

law of conservation of mass The principle that the total amount of matter is neither created nor destroyed during any chemical or physical change. (57)

limiting factor An environmental factor that causes a population to decrease in size. (42)

M

mutualism A type of symbiosis in which both species benefit from living together. (84)

N

natural resource Anything naturally occuring in the environment that humans use. (112)

niche How an organism makes its living and interacts with the biotic and abiotic factors in its habitat. (80)

O

organism A living thing. (37)

P

parasitism A type of symbiosis in which one organism lives with, on, or in a host and harms it. (86)

photosynthesis The process by which plants and other autotrophs capture and use light energy to make food from carbon dioxide and water. (6)

pioneer species The first species to populate an area during succession. (89)

population All the members of one species living in the same area. (39)

precipitation Any form of water that falls from clouds and reaches Earth's surface as rain, snow, sleet, or hail. (59)

predation An interaction in which one organism kills another for food or nutrients. (82)

producer An organism that can make its own food. (47)

S

succession The series of predictable changes that occur in a community over time. (89)

sustainability The ability of an ecosystem to maintain bioviersity and production indefinitely. (117)

symbiosis Any relationship in which two species live closely together and that benefits at least one of the species. (84)

INDEX

Page numbers for key terms are printed in boldface type.

INDEX

Page numbers for key terms are printed in boldface type.

T

U

V

W

CREDITS

Photographs

Photo locators denoted as follows: Top (T), Center (C), Bottom (B), Left (L), Right (R), Background (Bkgd)

Covers

Front Cover: Eirini Karapostoli/EyeEm/Getty Images
Back Cover: LHF Graphics/Shutterstock

Front Matter

iv: Clari Massimiliano/Shutterstock; vi: Grobler du Preez/Shutterstock; vii: Brian J. Skerry/National Geographic/Getty Images; viii: Kong Act/Shutterstock; x: Brian J. Skerry/National Geographic/Getty Images; xi: Gary Meszaros/Science Source/Getty Images.

Topic 1

002 Bkgrd: Douglas Orton/Alamy Stock Photo; 002 TR: Studio2013/Fotolia; 004: Andrey Nekrasov/Image Quest Marine; 005: David Courtenay/Getty Images; 006 B: Leena Robinson/Alamy Stock Photo; 006 Bkgrd: Shutterstock; 006 C: ArtTDi/Shutterstock; 006 T: Charlie Summers/Nature Picture Library; 007: Tunde Gaspar/Shutterstock; 011: Sacramento Bee/ Florence Low ZUMA Press, Inc./Alamy Stock Photo; 013: Patrick T. Fallon/Bloomberg/Getty Images; 014 Bkgrd: John Raoux/AP Photo; 014 TL: Rich Carey/iStock/Getty Images; 014 BL: John Raoux/AP Photo; 016: Michael Reusse/Getty Images; 017: Melinda Fawver/Shutterstock; 021 BL: Ramon Espelt/AGE Fotostock; 021 CL: Ramon Espelt/AGE Fotostock; 021 TL: Ramon Espelt/AGE Fotostock; 023 Bkgrd: Elena Schweitzer/Shutterstock; 023 BR: M. Unal Ozmen/Shutterstock; 028: Anne Ackermann/Getty Images; 029 BR: Martin Shields/Alamy Stock Photo; 029 CR: Chris Mattison/FLPA/Science Source;

Topic 2

032: Brian J Skerry/Getty Images; 034: Helen H Richardson/Getty Images; 036: Getty Images; 038: Ephotocorp/Alamy Stock Photo; 041: Martin Harvey/Alamy Stock Photo; 042: Awie Badenhorst/Alamy Stock Photo; 044: Steve Byland/Shutterstock; 046: Fritz Rauschenbach/Getty Images; 053: Oliver Smart/Alamy Stock Photo; 055 Bkgrd: Christpher Berkey/Alamy Stock Photo; 055 CR: Shutterstock; 055 TR: Christoph Gertler/Bangor University; 056: SOMKIET POOMSIRIPAIBOON/Shutterstock; 058: Paul Lemke/Fotolia; 060 Bkgrd: Jovannig/Fotolia; 060 BL: Cvalle/Shutterstock; 060 BR: Aleksander Bolbot/Getty Images; 061 BC: Blickwinkel/Alamy Stock Photo; 061 BL: Steven Widoff/Alamy Stock Photo; 061 BR: Yeko/Shutterstock; 065 B: JONATHAN PLANT/Alamy Stock Photo; 065 CR: Kuttelvaserova Stuchelova/Shutterstock; 065 T: Olha Insight/Shutterstock; 068 Bamboo: Gnek/Shutterstock; 068 Civet: Miroslav Chaloupka/Alamy Stock Photo; 068 Cobra: FLPAAlamy Stock Photo; 068 Douc: Bee eater/Shutterstock; 068 Dove: Luis Castaneda/Getty Images; 068 Fig: Sarama/Shutterstock; 068 Insect: Deposit Photos/Glow Images; 068 Jambu: David Bokuchava/Shutterstock; 068 Mango: Apiguide/Shutterstock; 068 Rhino: Terry Whittaker/Alamy Stock Photo; 068 Tiger: BIOSPHOTO/Alamy Stock Photo; 068 Viper: BIOSPHOTO/Alamy Stock Photo; 070: Mlorenz/Shutterstock; 071 L: GmbH/Alamy Stock Photo; 071 R: Loop Images Ltd/Alamy Stock Photo;

Topic 3

074: Shutterstock; 076: Skyward Kick Productions/Shutterstock; 078: Getty Images; 080: Frank Slack/Getty Images; 081 TC: Chloe Kaudeur/Getty Images; 081 TCR: Russell Burden/Getty Images; 081 TL: Alessio Frizziero/Getty Images; 081 TR: Steve Leach/Getty Images; 082: Horh/Fotolia; 084: Getty Images; 085 BR: Shaen Adey/Getty Images; 085 TR: Shutterstock; 086 BL: Alamy Stock Photo; 088: Erich Schmidt/Getty Images; 090 BL: Shutterstock; 090 TL: Alamy Stock Photo; 091 BR: Shutterstock; 091 T: Hellen Sergeyeva/Shutterstock; 094: Alamy Stock Photo; 095 B: Jan Martin Will/Shutterstock; 095 TR: Shutterstock; 096: Elvis Antson/Shutterstock; 098: Boezie/Getty Images; 099: Ludmila Yilmaz/Shutterstock; 100: Frieda Ryckaert/Getty Images; 101: Paul & Paveena Mckenzie/Getty Images; 102: 2630ben/Shutterstock; 103 Bkgrd: Charles Knowles/Shutterstock; 103 BR: Zhai Jianlan; Xinhua/Alamy Stock Photo; 103 CL: Zeljko Radojko/Shutterstock; 103 CR: VCG/Getty Images; 103 TL: Georgy Rozov/Getty Images; 103 TR: William Silver/Shutterstock; 104 B: Stocktrek Images, Inc/Alamy Stock Photo; 104 T: Reinhard Dirscherl/Alamy Stock Photo; 105 BL: Michael Doolittle/Alamy Stock Photo; 105 BR: Goodluz/Shutterstock; 105 CR: Ariel Skelley/Getty Images; 106: Leonardo Gonzalez/Shutterstock; 108: Chris Fourie/Shutterstock; 110: Michael Jones/Alamy Stock Photo; 111: 123RF GB Ltd; 112 BC: Holbox/Shutterstock; 112 BL: Ammit Jack/Shutterstock; 112 BR: Kletr/Shutterstock; 112 C: PointImages/Shutterstock; 112 CL: Hero Images/Getty Images; 112 CR: Pink Candy/Shutterstock; 113: Melpomene/Shutterstock; 115: Pawe/Shutterstock; 116: Nik Wheeler/Alamy Stock Photo; 117: Michael Willis/Alamy Stock Photo; 119 B: Alamy Stock Photo; 119 T: Alamy Stock Photo; 125 BR: Getty Images; 125 T: Jose Bernat Bercete/Getty Images;

End Matter

128 BCL: Philippe Plailly & Elisabeth Daynes/Science Source; 128 BL: EHStockphoto/Shutterstock; 128 TCL: Cyndi Monaghan/Getty Images; 128 TL: Javier Larrea/AGE Fotostock; 129: WaterFrame/Alamy Stock Photo; 130: Africa Studio/Shutterstock; 131: Jeff Rotman/Alamy Stock Photo; 132: Grant Faint/Getty Images; 133: Ross Armstrong/Alamy Stock Photo; 134: Geoz/Alamy Stock Photo; 137: Martin Shields/Alamy Stock Photo; 138: Nicola Tree/Getty Images; 139: Regan Geeseman/NASA; 141: Pearson Education Ltd.; 142: Pearson Education Ltd.; 143 BR: Pearson Education Ltd.; 143 TR: Pearson Education Ltd.

Program graphics: ArtMari/Shutterstock; BeatWalk/Shutterstock; Irmun/Shutterstock; LHF Graphics/Shutterstock; Multigon/Shutterstock; Nikolaeva/Shutterstock; silm/Shutterstock; Undrey/Shutterstock

Take Notes

Use this space for recording notes and sketching out ideas.

Take Notes

Use this space for recording notes and sketching out ideas.

Take Notes

Use this space for recording notes and sketching out ideas.

Take Notes

Use this space for recording notes and sketching out ideas.

Take Notes

Use this space for recording notes and sketching out ideas.

Take Notes

Use this space for recording notes and sketching out ideas.